First World War
and Army of Occupation
War Diary
France, Belgium and Germany

24 DIVISION
Headquarters, Branches and Services
Royal Army Veterinary Corps
Assistant Director Veterinary Services
21 August 1915 - 28 February 1919

WO95/2196/4

The Naval & Military Press Ltd
www.nmarchive.com
Published in association with The National Archives

Published by

The Naval & Military Press Ltd

Unit 10 Ridgewood Industrial Park,

Uckfield, East Sussex,

TN22 5QE England

Tel: +44 (0) 1825 749494

www.naval-military-press.com

www.nmarchive.com

This diary has been reprinted in facsimile from the original. Any imperfections are inevitably reproduced and the quality may fall short of modern type and cartographic standards.

© Crown Copyright
Images reproduced by permission of The National Archives, London, England, 2015.

Contents

Document type	Place/Title	Date From	Date To
Miscellaneous	WO95/2196-4		
Heading	24th Division Divl Troops Asst Dir Vety Services Aug 1915-Feb 1919		
Heading	24th Division H.Q. 24th Division Vol I Sept 15 Feb 19		
Heading	War Diary Of A D V S. 24 Division From 21/8/15 To 30-9-15 (Volume I)		
War Diary	Blackdown	21/08/1915	30/08/1915
War Diary	Montreuil	31/08/1915	31/08/1915
War Diary	Royons	01/09/1915	20/09/1915
War Diary	Bomy	21/09/1915	21/09/1915
War Diary	Busnes	22/09/1915	23/09/1915
War Diary	Bethune	24/09/1915	25/09/1915
War Diary	Sailly-Labourse	25/09/1915	28/09/1915
War Diary	St Hilaire	29/09/1915	30/09/1915
Heading	H.Q. 24th Div N.D. V.S. Vol 2 Oct 15		
Heading	War Diary Of A.D.V.S. 24th Division From 1-10-15 To 31-10-15 Volume (2)		
War Diary	St Hilaire	02/10/1915	02/10/1915
War Diary	Steenvoorde	02/10/1915	05/10/1915
War Diary	Reninghelst	06/10/1915	31/10/1915
Heading	A.D.V.S. 24th Div, Vol. 3 Nov 15		
Heading	War Diary Of A D V S. 24th Division From 1/11/15 To 30/11/15 Volume (3)		
War Diary	Reninghelst	01/11/1915	22/11/1915
War Diary	Tilqucs	23/11/1915	30/11/1915
Heading	A.D.B 24th Div. Vol: 4		
Heading	War Diary Of A D V S 24th Division From 1-12-15 To 31-12-15 Volume (4)		
War Diary	Tilques	01/12/1915	31/12/1915
Heading	A.D.V.S. 21st Div Vol 5. Jan		
Heading	War Diary Of A.D.V.S. 24th Division From 1.1.16 To 31.1.16 Volume (5)		
War Diary	Tilques	02/01/1916	07/01/1916
War Diary	Steenvoorde	07/01/1916	07/01/1916
War Diary	Reninghelst	08/01/1916	31/01/1916
Miscellaneous	A.D.V.S. 24th Div. Vol. 6		
Heading	War Diary Of A D V S. 24th Division From 1.2.16 To 29.2.16 Volume (6)		
War Diary	Reninghelst	01/02/1916	09/02/1916
War Diary	Boulogne	10/02/1916	10/02/1916
War Diary	Reninghelst	11/02/1916	29/02/1916
Heading	War Diary Of A D V S. 24th Division From 1.3.16 To 31.3.16 Volume (7)		
War Diary	Reninghelst	01/03/1916	21/03/1916
War Diary	Fletre	22/03/1916	30/03/1916
War Diary	St Jans Cappel	30/03/1916	31/03/1916
Heading	War Diary Of A D V S. 24th Division From 1.4.16 To 30.4.16 Volume (8)		
War Diary	St Jans Cappel	01/04/1916	17/04/1916
War Diary	St Jans Cappel Bailleul	18/04/1916	19/04/1916

War Diary	Bailleul	19/04/1916	30/04/1916
Heading	War Diary Of A D V S. 24th Division From 1.5.16 To 31.5.16 Volume (9)		
War Diary	Bailleul	01/05/1916	31/05/1916
Heading	War Diary Of A.D.V.S. 24th Division From 1.6.16 To 30.6.16 Volume 10.		
War Diary	Bailleul	01/06/1916	30/06/1916
Heading	War Diary Of A.D.V.S. 24th Division From 1-7-16 To 31-7-16 Volume 11.		
War Diary	Bailleul	01/07/1916	04/07/1916
War Diary	Locre	04/07/1916	10/07/1916
War Diary	Bailleul	11/07/1916	19/07/1916
War Diary	St Jans Cappel	20/07/1916	24/07/1916
War Diary	St Jans Cappel Amiens	24/07/1916	24/07/1916
War Diary	Amiens	25/07/1916	25/07/1916
War Diary	Cavillon	26/07/1916	31/07/1916
War Diary	Corbie	31/07/1916	31/07/1916
Heading	War Diary Of A.D.V.S. 24th Division From 1-8-16 To 31-8-16 Volume (12)		
War Diary	Corbie	01/08/1916	02/08/1916
War Diary	Forked Tree	02/08/1916	12/08/1916
War Diary	Citadel	13/08/1916	23/08/1916
War Diary	Forked Tree	24/08/1916	24/08/1916
War Diary	Buire	25/08/1916	30/08/1916
War Diary	E11 Central	31/08/1916	31/08/1916
Heading	War Diary Of A.D.V.S. 24th Division From 1-9-16 To 30-9-16 Volume 13		
War Diary	E11 Central	01/09/1916	06/09/1916
War Diary	Ailly Le Haut Clocher	07/09/1916	18/09/1916
War Diary	Bruay	19/09/1916	25/09/1916
War Diary	Camblain L'Abbe	26/09/1916	30/09/1916
Heading	War Diary Of A.D.V.S. 24th Division From 1-10-16 To 31-10-16 Volume 14		
War Diary	Camblain L'Abbe	01/10/1916	27/10/1916
War Diary	Bruay	28/10/1916	29/10/1916
War Diary	Braquemont	30/10/1916	31/10/1916
Heading	War Diary Of A.D.V.S. 24th Division From 1-11-16 To 30-11-16 Vol. (15)		
War Diary	Braquemont	01/11/1916	30/11/1916
Heading	War Diary Of A.D.V.S. 24th Division From. 1-12-16 To 31-12-16 Vol. 16		
War Diary	Braquemont	01/12/1916	31/12/1916
Heading	36th Div. Ret. Sect Vol: 5		
Heading	War Diary Of A.D.V.S. 24th Division From 1-1-17 To 31-1-17 Vol 17		
War Diary	Braquemont	01/01/1917	31/01/1917
Heading	War Diary Of A.D.V.S. 24th Division From 1-2-17 To 28-2-17 Vol. 18		
War Diary	Braquemont	01/02/1917	12/02/1917
War Diary	Labeuvriere	13/02/1917	28/02/1917
Heading	War Diary Of A.D.V.S. 24th Division From. 1-3-17 To 31-3-17 Vol. 19		
War Diary	Labeuvriere	01/03/1917	04/03/1917
War Diary	Barlin	05/03/1917	31/03/1917
Heading	War Diary Of A.D.V.S. 24th Division From 1-4-17 To 30-4-17 Vol. 20		

War Diary	Barlin	01/04/1917	02/04/1917
War Diary	Braquemont	03/04/1917	19/04/1917
War Diary	Norrent Fontes	20/04/1917	23/04/1917
War Diary	Bomy	24/04/1917	30/04/1917
Heading	War Diary Of A.D.V.S. 24th Division From 1-5-17 To 31-5-17 Vol 21		
War Diary	Bomy	01/05/1917	09/05/1917
War Diary	Norrent Fontes	10/05/1917	12/05/1917
War Diary	Droglandt	12/05/1917	15/05/1917
War Diary	Brandhoek	16/05/1917	17/05/1917
War Diary	Brandhoek	18/05/1917	29/05/1917
War Diary	Reninghelst	30/05/1917	31/05/1917
Heading	War Diary Of D.A.D.V.S. 24th Division From 1-6-17 To 30-6-17 Vol. 22		
War Diary	Reninghelst	01/06/1917	13/06/1917
War Diary	H31 b 5.2	14/06/1917	14/06/1917
War Diary	H31 B5.2 (28)	14/06/1917	15/06/1917
War Diary	H31 b 5.2 (Sheet 28)	16/06/1917	28/06/1917
War Diary	Caestre	29/06/1917	29/06/1917
War Diary	Lumbres	30/06/1917	30/06/1917
Heading	War Diary Of D.A.D.V.S. 24th Division From 1-7-17 To 31-7-17 Vol. 23		
War Diary	Lumbres	01/07/1917	19/07/1917
War Diary	Steenevoorde	19/07/1917	23/07/1917
War Diary	Zevecoten	23/07/1917	31/07/1917
Heading	War Diary Of D.A.D.V.S. 24th Division From 1-8-17 To 31-8-17 Vol. 24		
War Diary	Zevecoten	01/08/1917	31/08/1917
Heading	War Diary Of D.A.D.V.S. 24th Division From 1-9-17 To 30-9-17 Vol. 25		
War Diary	Zevecoten	01/09/1917	15/09/1917
War Diary	Merris	15/09/1917	20/09/1917
War Diary	I34a3.7 (Sheet 57c)	20/09/1917	27/09/1917
War Diary	Peronne	27/09/1917	29/09/1917
War Diary	Nobescourt Farm K32 Cent (62c)	30/09/1917	30/09/1917
Heading	War Diary Of D.A.D.V.S. 24th Division From 1-10-17 To 31-10-17 Vol. 26		
War Diary	Nobescourt Farm K32 Cent. (Sheet 62c)	01/10/1917	02/10/1917
War Diary	Nobescourt Farm K32 Central (62c)	02/10/1917	31/10/1917
Heading	War Diary Of D.A.D.V.S. 24th Division From 1-11-17 To 30-11-17 Vol. 27		
War Diary	Nobescourt Farm (K32 C. 62c)	01/11/1917	30/11/1917
Heading	War Diary Of D.A.D.V.S. 24th Division From 1-12-17 To 31-12-17 Vol. 28.		
War Diary	Nobescourt Farm (K32b. 62c)	01/12/1917	31/12/1917
Heading	War Diary Of D.A.D.V.S. 24th Division From 1-1-18 To 31-1-18 Vol 29		
War Diary	Nobescourt Farm (K 32b Sheet 62c)	01/01/1918	31/01/1918
Heading	War Diary Of D.A.D.V.S. 24th Division From 1-2-18 To 28-2-18 Vol. 30		
War Diary	Nobescourt Farm	01/02/1918	28/02/1918
Heading	War Diary Of D.A.D.V.S. 24th Division From 1-3-18 To 31-3-18 Vol. 31		
War Diary	Nobescourt Farm	01/03/1918	02/03/1918
War Diary	Flammicourt	03/03/1918	13/03/1918
War Diary	Bouvincourt	14/03/1918	22/03/1918

War Diary	Brie	23/03/1918	23/03/1918
War Diary	Hallu	24/03/1918	24/03/1918
War Diary	Rosieres	25/03/1918	31/03/1918
Heading	War Diary Of D.A.D.V.S. 24th Division From 1-4-18 To 30-4-18 Vol. 32		
War Diary	Cottenchy	01/04/1918	06/04/1918
War Diary	St Valery-Sur-Somme	07/04/1918	18/04/1918
War Diary	Lathieuloye	19/04/1918	03/05/1918
War Diary	Sains-En-Gohelle	04/05/1918	31/05/1918
Heading	War Diary Of D.A.D.V.S. 24th Division From 1-6-18 To 30-6-18 Vol. 34		
War Diary	Sains-En-Gohelle	01/06/1918	30/06/1918
Heading	War Diary Of D.A.D.V.S. 24th Division From 1-7-18 To 31-7-18 Vol 35		
War Diary	Sains En Gohelle	01/07/1918	31/07/1918
Heading	War Diary Of D.A.D.V.S. 24th Division From 1-8-18 To 31-8-18 Vol. 36		
War Diary	Sains-En-Gohelle	01/08/1918	31/08/1918
Miscellaneous War Diary	Horse Mastership Condition Of Animals		
Heading	War Diary Of D.A.D.V.S. 24th Division From 1-9-18 To 30-9-18 Vol. 37		
War Diary	Sains-En-Gohelle	01/09/1918	30/09/1918
Heading	War Diary Of D.A.D.V.S. 24th Division From 1-10-18 To 31-10-18 Vol. 38		
War Diary	Lucheux	01/10/1918	06/10/1918
War Diary	Moeuvres	07/10/1918	08/10/1918
War Diary	Rumilly	09/10/1918	09/10/1918
War Diary	E. Subirts Of Cambrai	10/10/1918	13/10/1918
War Diary	Avesnes-Lez-Aubert	14/10/1918	18/10/1918
War Diary	Cambrai	19/10/1918	25/10/1918
War Diary	St Aubert	26/10/1918	31/10/1918
Heading	War Diary Of D.A.D.V.S. 24th Division From. 1-11-18 To 30-11-18 Vol. 39		
War Diary	St. Aubert	01/11/1918	03/11/1918
War Diary	Bermerain	04/11/1918	04/11/1918
War Diary	Sepmeries	05/11/1918	05/11/1918
War Diary	Wargnies-Le Grand	06/11/1918	09/11/1918
War Diary	Bavay	10/11/1918	18/11/1918
War Diary	Masny	19/11/1918	26/11/1918
War Diary	Sameon	27/11/1918	30/11/1918
Heading	War Diary Of D.A.D.V.S. 24th Division From 1-12-18 To 31-12-18 Vol 40		
War Diary	Sameon	01/12/1918	12/12/1918
War Diary	Rongy	13/12/1918	18/12/1918
War Diary	Tournai	19/12/1918	31/12/1918
Heading	War Diary Of D.A.D.V.S. 24th Division From 1-1-19 To 31-1-19 Vol. 41		
War Diary	Tournai	01/01/1919	31/01/1919
Heading	War Diary Of D.A.D.V.S. 24th Division From 1-2-19 To 28-2-19 Vol. 42		
War Diary	Tournai	01/02/1919	28/02/1919

WO 95/21961/4

24TH DIVISION
DIVL TROOPS

ASST DIR VETY SERVICES
AUG 1915 - FEB 1919

121/7083

24th Division

H.Q. 24th Division A.D.V.S.
Vol I Sept. 15 — Feb. 19

Confidential

War Diary of.
   A.D.V.S. 24ᵗʰ DIVISION.

from 21/8/15   To 30-9-15.

(Volume. I)

Army Form C. 2118

WAR DIARY
or
INTELLIGENCE SUMMARY.
(Erase heading not required.)

Instructions regarding War Diaries and Intelligence Summaries are contained in F. S. Regs., Part II. and the Staff Manual respectively. Title pages will be prepared in manuscript.

Hour, Date, Place	Summary of Events and Information	Remarks and References to Appendices
21/- BLACKDOWN 22-27/8/15	Orders for mobilization received. Inspected Units and commenced examining animals until k. process received.	
27/8/15 "	Received orders from Q.M.G. Division to proceed to Southampton on 29" inst.	
28/8/15 "	Visited No 3b. Mobile Veterinary Section and issued instructions regarding disposal of Sick and lame after my departure. Arranged with A.D.V.S. A.C. reference handing over of Pharmacy at DEEPCUT. Reported departure to A.D.V.S. A.C.	
29/8/15 "	Proceeded to Southampton with H.Q. animals and details and embarked en route for LE HAVRE. At Southampton some animals I had condition. Talk with Hallein, and applied with very hoove horses fit for work were not allowed to embark by Te Veterinary Officer on inspection duty. Some of these animals were not replaced & those that were had no medium of having been taken with Hallein.	
30/8/15 "	Arrived LE HAVRE. No casualties on route. animals housed same evening.	

Army Form C. 2118

WAR DIARY
or
INTELLIGENCE SUMMARY.
(Erase heading not required.)

Instructions regarding War Diaries and Intelligence Summaries are contained in F. S. Regs., Part II. and the Staff Manual respectively. Title pages will be prepared in manuscript.

Hour, Date, Place	Summary of Events and Information	Remarks and References to Appendices
31/5 MONTREUIL	Arrived MONTREUIL. Orders for proceeding to destination here do report but no one knew where to go. So the men and animals were billeted for the night at NEUVILLE.	
1 9/15 ROYONS	Arrived at ROYONS, H.Q of the XXIV Division. Found distribution of units difficult to arrange for the attendance of Veterinary Officers. The Divisional area is 16 miles across and Veterinary Officers arrived in FRANCE police France in accordance with instructions contained in War Establishment, Part III New Armies. As the troops are of Artillery were together, and in few adjoining parties of the front area comprising the Division.	
2 9/15	Visited Bread with a view to attaching units to Veterinary Officers.	
3 9/15	Arranged for Veterinary attendance on a unit of Division, and informed Veterinary Officers.	
4 9/15	Visited Lieuts MACGREGOR, DOBIE, and DODWORTH A.V.C. informed they knew this area. The other Veterinary Officers had not yet arrived. Explained the principles of training in the Field and demonstrated Goods Animals.	

WAR DIARY
of
INTELLIGENCE SUMMARY.
(Erase heading not required.)

Army Form C. 2118.

Hour, Date, Place	Summary of Events and Information	Remarks and References to Appendices
9/15 ROYONS	36 Mobile Veterinary Section arrived, and proceeded to NEUVILLE.	
5/15 "	Mobile Veterinary Section had been billetted at NEUVILLE. Went to look for them. Personally visited arrangements for men & horses from BEAURAINVILLE near Rail head and to cache of Thrashed huts area.	
6/15 "	Section arrived BEAURAINVILLE. Visited Capt. W.K. Bann. AVC(T.F) the C.O. and explained the method of conducting an R. arrival and departure, and replied the Veterinary Officer that the Section was ready to receive Sick animals.	
7/15 "	Visited 72, 73 & 74 Field Ambulances. These units have not completely Arrived one to change of plan arrived, but a transport Officer Fred. Field Ambulance had to go to hospital as the Officer R.A.M.C. to him had to know nothing whatever of animal management.	

WAR DIARY
or
INTELLIGENCE SUMMARY.
(Erase heading not required.)

Army Form C. 2118

Hour, Date, Place	Summary of Events and Information	Remarks and References to Appendices
ROYONS 7/9/15	A Trained Transport Officer from A.S.C. attached Bdes. Units met with Chance Brigadier's efficiency between Officer's & always have been holding forage item every supplies for their area are so large that they cannot spare & time their units require.	
ROYONS 9/9/15	Lieut T.F. DONWORTH proceeded h/k 108 and 108 Bde R.F.A. for gun practice and to temporarily attached from the Division.	
ROYONS 10/9/15	Lieut L.H. LEACH proceeded with 109 and 10 7 Bder R.F.A. for gun practice and is temporarily attached from the Division. During the departure of these officers Lieut M.A. Macgregor was attached totake the duties of Lieut DONWORTH left behind in addition to his own duties. Capt W.R. Barron emerged from between attendance on Units in vicinity of little between section.	
ROYONS 11/9/15	Saw R.T.O BEAR RAINVILLE absence departed g/g Rainville & Base.	
ROYONS 12/9/15	16 animals sent to between to hospital. ABBEVILLE via Railway. Sec. animals overall forged and entrained.	

WAR DIARY
or
INTELLIGENCE SUMMARY.
(Erase heading not required.)

Army Form C. 2118.

Hour, Date, Place	Summary of Events and Information	Remarks and references to Appendices
12/15 9/15 ROYONS	Instructions issued for Servicemen Cmdt Bulls and Officers & Orderlies on Technical Check issued in ENGLAND did not contain these articles. Visited Mobile Veterinary Section, tried smoke-helmets on horses and mules.	
13/15 ROYONS	Divisional Ammunition Column left 6/10am R.F.A. Brigades with earlier Division. No information had given time about the movement of the unit. Inspected Spare Transport of 17 to 73 "Brigade, animals were well looked after and Transport Officers had attention to their duties. Recommend (1) A.A.Cliff be used. They take out water equivalent arrangement.	
14/15 9/15 ROYONS	Visited Mobile Veterinary Section, found animals sent in by hick without veterinary recommendation of while attached horse motivated testy this practice. Inspected Spare transport of 11" Essex and 8" Bedfords. Pointed to D.V.S. that the Motor Car for A.D.V.S. has been appropriated most distant in for No1 Stretcherbearer's Mail VIII New Arrival. Owing to want of appearance of Officers A.V.C. in his Division + make sure service the mail of his car affects the proper performance of any duties.	

Army Form C. 2118.

WAR DIARY
or
INTELLIGENCE SUMMARY.
(Erase heading not required.)

Instructions regarding War Diaries and Intelligence Summaries are contained in F.S. Regs., Part II. and the Staff Manual respectively. Title pages will be prepared in manuscript.

Hour, Date, Place	Summary of Events and Information	Remarks and references to Appendices
15/9/15 ROYONS	Inspected R.E. Field Companies. Demonstrated method of bandaging heel. Ensure the heel protection & prevention of necrosis and Tetanus.	
16/9/15 ROYONS	Inspected Glasgow Yeomanry, found several cases & ploughing of tails, due to trotting when knee-cases overseas. Told C.O. not to allow any more trotting of tails. Visited Mobile Veterinary Section, and the crew track to this brink to fit for work, and arranged for the evacuation of remainder of cases.	
17/9/15 ROYONS 18/9/15 ROYONS	16 cases evacuated to ABBEVILLE. Proceeded to No.1 Advanced Base Veterinary Stores, ABBEVILLE and drew Veterinary Stores for the Division.	
19/9/15 ROYONS	Visited Mobile Veterinary Section and arranged distribution of Veterinary Stores.	
20/9/15 ROYONS	Orders for Division to march on 23rd instant-issued. Two Veterinary Officers are attached from (a) Field Artillery Brigades & as the Division will march by two different routes, the remaining two Veterinary Officers here	

Army Form C. 2118.

WAR DIARY
or
INTELLIGENCE SUMMARY.
(Erase heading not required.)

Instructions regarding War Diaries and Intelligence Summaries are contained in F. S. Regs., Part II. and the Staff Manual respectively. Title pages will be prepared in manuscript.

Hour, Date, Place	Summary of Events and Information	Remarks and references to Appendices
20/9/15 ROYONS	here	
	posted to Mounted Brigade groups.	
	Mobile Veterinary Section arranged to evacuate sicklin (16) cases.	
21/9/15 BOMY	Arrived BOMY with D.H.Q. at 6 p.m.	
	Mobile Veterinary Section marches from BEAURAINVILLE to LAIRES	
22/9/15 BUSNES	Arrived BUSNES - 5 p.m. Mobile Veterinary Section arrived HAM-EN-ARTOIS. March with D/Orders instruction opening netting of dealing with animals necessarily left behind.	
23/9/15 BUSNES	Issued Goo Smoke Helmets to 1st & 2nd R.A. for distribution to Artillery Brigades.	
24/9/15 BETHUNE	Arrived BETHUNE 10 p.m. Mobile Veterinary Section arrived ANNEZIN.	
25/9/15 "	Visited Mobile Veterinary Section Arrangements of eight (8) evacuation.	
	Issued orders for Veterinary Officers to report into communication with the when they arrive at new places. Met D.D.V.S 1st Army and learnt Return list of horses left behind.	
	Division marches at preconcerted program into action.	
25/9/15 SAILLY-LABOURSE 11.30 p.m.	Left BETHUNE at 10 p.m. proceeded to LE RUTOIRE to A.H.Q.	

WAR DIARY or INTELLIGENCE SUMMARY

Army Form C. 2118.

Hour, Date, Place	Summary of Events and Information	Remarks and References to Appendices
25/9/15 SAILLY LABOURSE	Returned letter to H.Q.(Q Branch) at SAILLY LABOURSE.	
26/9/15 "	Met DDVS 1st Army, explained to him the difficulty of intercommunication with Veterinary Officers in the field, at King applied with information from Q.M.G. His intention was to Q. R.O 534 reference care of sick horses to D. Orders. Selected position for Mobile Veterinary Section. Sent orders & guide to Mobile Veterinary Section into after ascertaining eight (8) cases proceeded to place selected & informed V.Os. and units of the Division.	
27/9/15 "	Got into communication with and afterwards sent all V.O.'s horses & spares transport, Divisional train, and Ammunition Column. Sent in eight (8) horses and one mule to Veterinary Section. Section evacuated sixteen (16) cases. Met DDVS 1st Army told him Q.M.G. Aid Division accepted. Division would take R. horses	
28/9/15 "	for ADVS - Guards Division. R&R new tester site too difficult when worked in connection hill more.	

Army Form C. 2118.

WAR DIARY
or
INTELLIGENCE SUMMARY.
(Erase heading not required.)

Instructions regarding War Diaries and Intelligence Summaries are contained in F.S. Regs., Part II. and the Staff Manual respectively. Title pages will be prepared in manuscript.

Hour, Date, Place	Summary of Events and Information	Remarks and references to Appendices
28/9/15 SAILLY LABOURSE	Orders issued while to move to St HILAIRE. Arranged with section FANs when to be to guide section to billet.	
29/9/15 St HILAIRE	Shot informed R.A. Brigades when returning, left M.O. at disposal of 9th Divisional Artillery, supplied ndls to DDVS 1st Army. Arrived St HILAIRE.	
30/9/15 "	Orders issued for Division to hold itself in readiness to move. Mobile Veterinary Section evacuated to C[?] cases.	

121/7517.

H.Q. 24th Sig- M.S.V.S.
1st 2
Oct 15

CONFIDENTIAL

War Diary of

A.D.V.S. 24th Division.

From 1-10-15   to   31-10-15.

Volume (2)

Army Form C. 2118.

WAR DIARY - A.D.V.S. 24th Division.

INTELLIGENCE SUMMARY.

(Erase heading not required.)

Instructions regarding War Diaries and Intelligence Summaries are contained in F.S. Regs., Part II. and the Staff Manual respectively. Title pages will be prepared in manuscript.

Hour, Date, Place		Summary of Events and Information	Remarks and references to Appendices
ST HILAIRE	2.10.15 10 A.M.	Orders to move issued.	
STEENVOORDE	" 2 P.M.	Arrived STEENVOORDE. Men are very large bodies. it had difficult to prove veterinary attendance to all units with the present staff.	
		Have great difficulty in getting round the division as I am alone & fear had no A.D.V.S. being quite appropriated by A. D. O'Farrell of the division -	
"	5-10-15	Proceeded to RENINGHELST to select place for mobile Veterinary Section.	
RENINGHELST	6.10.15	Arrived RENINGHELST.	
"	8-10-15	Conference of Veterinary Officers - returns & Return. 25 Horses of 106 Bde R.F.A. sent to Mobile Veterinary Section for fever accompanying - rash had that they were cast. The R.O. No 97 2nd Army on this reported in Divisional Order & his Subject.	
"	10-10-15	Visited D.D.V.S. 2nd Army on his return - re Casting for the Rear.	

(9 29 6) W 2794 100,000 8/14 H W V Forms/C. 2118/11

WAR DIARY or INTELLIGENCE SUMMARY

Army Form C. 2118.

Hour, Date, Place	Summary of Events and Information	Remarks and references to Appendices
RENINGHELST 10.10.15 (contd.)	Veterinary reasons.	
" 11-10-15	Reptiles kept to veterinary animals from Mobile Veterinary Section held necessary creating arrivals as protected.	
" 12-10-15	Captain M.N. BARRON A.V.C (T.F) O/C 36 Mobile Veterinary Section on sick list - to hospital. Pending appointment further places o/c A.D.V.S. took charge Section.	
" 14-10-15	Field trip heavers by R.T.A. no means of shortening heels of shoes unless I little of the small sheen. The pole or shape of foot complete fitting. Reported to D.A.D.V.S. who moved about complete filling. Conference of Veterinary Officers of the Division.	
" 15-10-15		
" 16-10-15	Captain A.F. COLOMBE Canadian Veterinary Corps – 1st Canadian Division arrived for temporary command of 36 Mobile Veterinary Section, vice Captain M.N. BARRON A.V.C (T.F) evacuated–sick.	
" 18-10-15	17 cases evacuated by Section. S.E. 7706 Sergt. GIBSON D.W.T. M.C. transfered from B/108 Bde R.F.A to 24 D.A.C @ Vice S.E. 3535 Sergt BRACY A.J. A.V.C.	

Army Form C. 2118.

WAR DIARY
or
INTELLIGENCE SUMMARY.
(Erase heading not required.)

Hour, Date, Place	Summary of Events and Information	Remarks and references to Appendices
RENING-HELST 18.10.15 (Cont'd)		
" 20.10.15	Serjt BRACEY, A.J. M.C. reverted sick. Lance R.L.A. Behan hit his Veterinary Sergeant in the body as refusing to one him with clothes & threatening to turn him out of the Sergeants mess. The C.R.A. between to have matters & general behaviour of Mess Sergeant & he has given notice to sever him in currence.	by
" 21.10.15	Went out with O.C. Mobile Veterinary Section and on Sergeant and selected a site for an advance dressing & collecting Station. No.746 Serjeant Appleby. C.A.V.C posted to 36 M.Rifle Veterinary Section - vice S.E. 384 Pte Brodrick F.F. M.C. Vacated sick - on 18th inst.	by
" 22.10.15	Weekly Conference of V.O.'s of the division.	by
" 23.10.15	With reference to the posting of Serjt Appleby, vice Pte Brodrick application made to D.D.V.S. 2 Army for a private to place S/o Sergeant, the Section being up to strength as regards Sergeant.	by

WAR DIARY
or
INTELLIGENCE SUMMARY.

(Erase heading not required.)

Army Form C. 2118.

Hour, Date, Place	Summary of Events and Information	Remarks and references to Appendices
RENINGHELST. 24-X-15	Visited 36 Mobile Veterinary Section & arranged for drawing rattle & timber for making horse standings and shelter.	
" 26-X-15	16 animals presented by 36 Mobile Veterinary Section.	
" 27-X-15	D.D.V.S. 2nd Army called. Explained method of making horse rugs fit. The present issue are too large for Cobs & hyl. bac. Broads causing wounds on the withers.	
" 28-X-15	Lt. Bethie T.A. A.V.C. applied for 6 days Cadre leave. Directed his Charge (Lehren Zunk-dael, Dranoth) and have arrangement for the performance of his duties. Watkin - A.V.C. D.D.V.S. 2nd Army called with reference to transferring of Veteran at F.O.M.S. (Skipgrove) to A.V.C.	
" 29-X-15	Saw the C.R.A. reference transferring of F.O.M.S. 17 H.A.C. The C.R.A. stated that these H.Q.h.S. were enlisted because	

WAR DIARY
or
INTELLIGENCE SUMMARY

Army Form C. 2118.

(Erase heading not required.)

Hour, Date, Place	Summary of Events and Information	Remarks and references to Appendices
RENINGHELST 29/10/15 (cont'd)	because Farrier Sergeants have not available - had of they were transferred they mean to start feathering. Spinola but that his establishment has four Sergeant N.C.O. and also five Farrier Sergeants per brigade & that they were deficient of Farrier Sergeants & says there to promote from their Farrier staff. however as the C.O.A. cared not be convinced to uphold his established transfer had applied to the DDVS. 2nd Army.	
30.X.15	Lieut Irvine J.A. AVC invalided 17th Batt. of	
31.X.15	Visited DDVS. 2nd Army. at Herne Quarter regarding of transfer of TQMS (Shelgrove) to this A.V.C. of	

A.D.B. 24th Sir.
vol. 3

D/7795

Ans

Novr 15

Confidential

War Diary of.

A D V S, 24ᵈ Division.

From. 1"/15 To. 30"/15

Volume (3).

WAR DIARY ADVS. 24th DIVISION

Army Form C. 2118

INTELLIGENCE SUMMARY

Hour, Date, Place	Summary of Events and Information	Remarks and References to Appendices
RENINGHELST. 1.11.15	Lieut. J. Blackburn. A.V.C. arrived and proceeded to 107 Brigade R.F.A. and took charge of Mont. T.A. Dobie A.V.C. evacuated sick. Visited 36. Mobile Veterinary Section and sent arrivals for evacuation. DDVS. 2nd Army visited this office, also C.R.A. reference F.O.M.S. Stated he not communicate to ourselves later. No. 6042. Sergt. W. G. Candler. A.V.C. transferred to H.Q. 2nd Army. No. 88261.F.Q.M.S. (Shillyman). T. Cooper. allotted to B/107 Bde R.F.A. vice Sergt. W. G. Candler. A.V.C. Surgeon to A.V.C. issued with a copy of Animal Management. Lieut. J. H. Laurie. A.V.C. arrived and took on command of 36. Mobile Veterinary Section. Capt. A. E. Colombe. C.V.C. handed over command of 36. Mobile Veterinary Section, and returned same day to 1st Canadian Division.	
" 2.11.15	Visited 24 D.A.C. Camp re bad condition, recommended a new Camp to Q. Branch.	

Army Form C. 2118

WAR DIARY
or
INTELLIGENCE SUMMARY.
(Erase heading not required.)

Instructions regarding War Diaries and Intelligence Summaries are contained in F. S. Regs., Part II. and the Staff Manual respectively. Title pages will be prepared in manuscript.

Hour, Date, Place	Summary of Events and Information	Remarks and References to Appendices
RENINGHELST. 2.11.15 (Cont'd).	Visited Mobile Veterinary Section with a R.E. Officer regarding Stalling for Sick animals.	
" 4-11-15 (?)	Visited Nos. 1 & 2 Section D.A.C. Sent seven horses from No2 Section to Mobile Veterinary Section. No1. Section Casualty Ford. Animals poor. Gave V.O. the instruction to pick out all poor cases & part by themselves & inform me. Visited No1. Section D.A.C. from 36 horses from Cadre - hind leg. Rugs being any how - No NCO the general supervision lacking. Reported matter to D.D.V.S. 2nd Army.	
" 5-11-15	Monthly conference of V.O's.	
" 6-11-15	Went to Richelene with D.A.Q.M.G. for Remounts also Fort Willshe on N.E.O from Mobile Veterinary Section to take on hand Cathrest.	
" 8-11-15	34 Animals evacuated by Mobile Veterinary Section. 23 from No1. Section D.A.C. - these were seen by D.D.V.S. 2nd Army before evacuation. D.D.V.S. 2nd Army has over by D.D.V.S. 2nd Army inspected D.A.C. in the afternoon.	

WAR DIARY
INTELLIGENCE SUMMARY

Hour, Date, Place	Summary of Events and Information	Remarks and References to Appendices
RENINGHELST. 8.11.15 (Cont'd)	Reported on threats of Foot & Mouth Disease in an different localities, and instructions issued. Matter reported to DDVS, 2nd Army. Q Branch & Medical Authorities. In conjunction with S.C.M. Captain R.A. selected 180 Mules 9 good at	
" 9-11-15	Classes [condition] for service out of France. Reference transfer of F.O.M.S. 9 R.A. to A.V.C. Duty, Command are not assisting in this matter, & the F.O.M.S. Object [?] [?] at rear P.	
" 10.11.15	Visited Wagon lines 97 Belgian Artillery, recommence improvement Standings reported attention. Funds [?] sick animals. Mobile Veterinary Section Shelters for animals in course of erection. Cover for about 40 animals.	
" 11.11.15	Interview with DDVS - 2nd Army. Re CRA reference F/M transfer of F.O.M.S. to A.V.C. Object was explained CRA said he would be to pressure put a F.Q.M.S. either in my [?]	
" 12-11-15	hrestly, Expense of Veterinary Officers.	

Army Form C. 2118

WAR DIARY
or
INTELLIGENCE SUMMARY.
(Erase heading not required.)

Instructions regarding War Diaries and Intelligence Summaries are contained in F. S. Regs., Part II. and the Staff Manual respectively. Title pages will be prepared in manuscript.

Hour, Date, Place	Summary of Events and Information	Remarks and References to Appendices
RENINGHELST. 13-11-15	Visited 1st DAC and 108 Bde R.F.A. with Staff Captain R.A. Selected Mules for service out of France.	
" 14-11-15	Visited 196 Coy. A.S.C. with regard to case of horse - people so far disposed miserably & arranged precautions. Appealed to have an order to Mobile Veterinary Section. Visited Farm occupied by H.Q. 107 Bde R.F.A. - Saw some supposed cases of foot-and-Mouth Disease. Forwarded report to D.D.V.S. 2nd Army on proposed reduction of the Divisional G.S. horses from Mobile Veterinary Section. Zone Title (A.F. C.1098) neight amount to 15 divisional horses by regulars. Article are very badly equipped not to conduct in any horse accommodation. If the Divisional G.S. horses in taken away it would entail a reduction of stores & impair the working efficiency of the Section.	
" 15-11-15	Visited 3rd & 7th Belgian Field Artillery near VLAMERTINGHE at	
" 16-11-15	Went to GODANAERSVELDT Station. Railhead. Saw Mobile	

WAR DIARY
INTELLIGENCE SUMMARY.
(Erase heading not required.)

Army Form C. 2118.

Hour, Date, Place		Summary of Events and Information	Remarks and References to Appendices
RENINGHELST.	16.11.15 (cont'd)	Mobile Veterinary Section ordered 14 sick animals for Base. One sick horse left with 74 Field Ambulance. BOESCHEPE, unable to proceed at Inspected Horses sent in exchange for Mules from Indian Corps	
"	17-11-15	at 108, 109 Brigade Ammunition Columns and 24th D.A.C. at	
"	18-11-15	Field Mobile Veterinary Section, running to ascertain regarding horses of the division. Have G.R.O. No 534 "Horses, Sick, Care of" referred to D. orders	
"	19-11-15	Health, Conference Veterinary Officers & gave instructions regarding sick cases unable to march — was toget into Communication with him on arrival at new destination at	
"	21-11-15	Saw to a movement of animals on march to Transport to the officers at request of G.O.C. Division — 50 animals exercised by Mobile Veterinary Section.	
"	22-11-15	V.O.'s march with their R.F.A. Brigades on officer with Divisional train Mobile Veterinary Section with Field Artillery & approved to TILQUES.	

Army Form C. 2118

WAR DIARY
or
INTELLIGENCE SUMMARY.
(Erase heading not required.)

Instructions regarding War Diaries and Intelligence Summaries are contained in F. S. Regs., Part II. and the Staff Manual respectively. Title pages will be prepared in manuscript.

Hour, Date, Place	Summary of Events and Information	Remarks and References to Appendices
RENINGHELST - 22-11-15 (Cont.)		
A.M.	Left RENINGHELST.	
P.M.	Arrive TILQUES. reported office at 6.45 p.m. at TILQUES. Inspected billets & animals to 36 Mobile Veterinary Section.	
TILQUES 23-11-15	O.C. Division visited Office & arranged for future transport of RA & other Officers on Animal Management.	
" 24-11-15		
" 25-11-15	Visited 73 B. Brigade. 73 Field Am[bulance] at EPERLECQUES. also DHQ. that Prussia Arrived - Report Company Rd., Glasgow Germany at TILQUES.	
" 26-11-15	Arranged for Cost [?] learning French Whilst here. This morning am informed none available. Those on week's other officers can for ADVS. with War Establishment Part III - [?] available. In reply from D.V.S. not received from what appears use of Cost during September. Mobile Veterinary Section arrived TILQUES at	
" 27-11-15	Perused area [?] mail. receipt R[?] from Q Branch.	

WAR DIARY
or
INTELLIGENCE SUMMARY.
(Erase heading not required.)

Hour, Date, Place	Summary of Events and Information	Remarks and References to Appendices
TILQUES 27-11-15 (Cn10)	Visited 17th Infantry Brigade tren. 103. 104th Field Conference RE, 74 Field Ambulance and 19th Company ASC at	
" 28-11-15	Visited Glasgow Yeomanry — arranged programme for trial ADDVS - 2nd Army on 29th inst. at	
" 29-11-15	DDVS 2nd Army spoke of am hopeing 36 Mobile Veterinary Section. Glasgow Yeomanry and the Company ASC at	
" 30-11-15	Had attention called to D.O. to DRO 269 d 16-10-15. reference clipping Mules, also GRO 301-399 reference Ind. Cavs. Visited 107 Brigade R.F.A. at	

A.S.B. 24th 8bris.
Vol: 4

7897/
131

V.511.

<u>Confidential</u>.

WAR DIARY of

ADVS. 24ᵗʰ DIVISION.

FROM 1-12-15 TO 31-12-15.

Volume. (4).

Army Form C. 2118.

WAR DIARY ADVS
INTELLIGENCE SUMMARY. 24th DIVISION
(Erase heading not required.)

Instructions regarding War Diaries and Intelligence Summaries are contained in F. S. Regs., Part II. and the Staff Manual respectively. Title pages will be prepared in manuscript.

Hour, Date, Place	Summary of Events and Information	Remarks and references to Appendices
TILQUES 1-12-15	Visited 24th Divisional Ammunition Column at	
" 2-12-15	Visited Divisional Technical Point arranged for lectures to be given on Animal Management at	
" 3-12-15	Accompanied DDR 2nd Army round Divisions and inspected animals for rest and eating. Found several horses 16, 17 and 18 years old, these have very long been been evacuated etc.	

Army Form C. 2118.

WAR DIARY
or
INTELLIGENCE SUMMARY.
(Erase heading not required.)

Instructions regarding War Diaries and Intelligence
Summaries are contained in F. S. Regs., Part II.
and the Staff Manual respectively. Title pages
will be prepared in manuscript.

Hour, Date, Place	Summary of Events and Information	Remarks and References to Appendices
TILQUES. 3-12-15 (cont'd)	Animals Front went Cutting- Front horses from 16, 17, 18 y on ret, horses being kept new exercised at	
" 4-12-15	DDVS- 2nd Army accompanied by MVS to Brig: Inspected 104 Brigade R.F.A. and 2nd D.A.C. Remarks on Area- Difficulty of finding recommending Horse-Forced unit. Position of those horses in 2nd Brigade feeling Picketing poor Near Forge Pitons officers Hy Arty. Net- Clipping grounds. Recommended fuel Standard for Hors Section D.A.C. left exposed at Hand. refer site to 9 Bde R.F.A. + 2nd D.A.C. at	
" 5-12-15 P.h.	Wikia pres. Visited 196 Company A.S.C. informed here available. Visited 196 Cory A.S.C.- Found very itchy horse- ho parasite on Saminsohir- Arrived scrabies.	
" 6-12-15	Visited Zleinoline- Case of Parsplic Mange (Mud per microscope) Animal evacuated with Mesanthe taken.	
" 9-12-15 P.h.	Lecture on Animal Management to Divisional Technical School Parkeri Evacuation from 36 Mble Veterinary Section, including two	

(9296) W 2294 100,000 S/14 H W V Forms/C. 2118/11.

WAR DIARY
or
INTELLIGENCE SUMMARY.
(Erase heading not required.)

Army Form C. 2118.

Hour, Date, Place	Summary of Events and Information	Remarks and References to Appendices
TILQUES. 9-12-15 (to 11-12-15)	Including	
" 11-12-15	No cases of Anaphylaxis Horse (2 Denials and 19th Company ASC)	
" 13-12-15	V.O.'s worked at Office. Prepared weekly return. Thirty-four evacuations from 36 Mobile Veterinary Section (includes nine Cast animals - Nineteen(?) cases) & this Case of Anaphylaxis Horse from 194 Company ASC	
" 15-12-15	Visited 73 Field Ambulance & found a deficiency of Horse-rugs — no evident cause.	
" 16-12-15	Visited 108 & 109 Brigade R.F.A. and 194 Company ASC at	
" 17-12-15	Weekly Conference P.V.O's. Visited DADVS with reference to the supply of Horse rugs, they ask our first Shoes, etc. at	
" 18-12-15	Visited 105 Bde R.F.A.	
" 19-12-15	Visited 73 and 72 Infantry Brigades. One suspected mange encounter from No.2 Sec. FA.C. - no parasites found in scrapings.	
" 20-12-15	Visited 04 F.A.C. Saw animals Cobat Cases - Sarcoptic scabies by the Matt. Visited 194 & 194 Companies ASC.	
" 22-12-15	Visited 19th Cy MSC inspected a suspicious case [mange?]	

WAR DIARY
or
INTELLIGENCE SUMMARY.
(Erase heading not required.)

Army Form C. 2118.

Hour, Date, Place	Summary of Events and Information	Remarks and References to Appendices
TILQUES 22.12.15 (Cont'd)	next	
23.12.15	Company titles taken prior to Parade. Lt. Central inspecting Officer may relax all precautions taken.	
	Gave lecture on Animal Management to Officers & N.C.O.'s of Coast at Divisional School.	
	Visited Chargers Zonnerany.	
24.12.15	V.O.'s attended Veterinary Conference - Special attention called to inoculating horses on the trench vaccination to transport Officers whom reporting animals unsuitable left behind in line of march.	
25.12.15	Visited 105 Bde R.F.A.	
9.pm.	Orders for horse suspended.	
11.30pm	Orders for same cancelled.	
26.12.15	Visited Rail Head at WATTEN where 36 Mobile Veterinary Section unrailed 30 animals from 2nd Division and 73 from other formations of Divisional Trains.	
27.12.15	Visited DHQ Transport lines - Signal Company, H.Q. Divisional Train	

WAR DIARY
INTELLIGENCE SUMMARY

Hour, Date, Place	Summary of Events and Information	Remarks and References to Appendices
YPRES. 27-12-15 (Cont'd) and 28-12-15	Chagos Summary of Visited 7th Infantry Brigade area and inspected Infantry transport, front defences, Horse Masts, Dug outs, Montages at Brigade Faynd Section, wounded where DC Divisional Signal Company. Applied for CinC forward OR.A. and 109 Brigade R.F.A. at 9. am on 29 "inst." of	
29-12-15	to cut down, rig ups to my official application. A/c to AA + QMG regarding leave for Veterinary personnel. Visited Moulle regarding fetheral of 1st month divorce, reported actg for Division. Château hut occupied by Postal Corps of DDVS. 2nd Army visited Ypres, Inspected 36 Mobile Veterinary Section.	

WAR DIARY
INTELLIGENCE SUMMARY.
(Erase heading not required.)

Hour, Date, Place	Summary of Events and Information	Remarks and References to Appendices
ILQUES. 29.12.15 (Cont'd)	DDVS - 2 Army interviewed Sergt-Major A.V.C. with attached 107 mesne R.F.A. men attached. 3 Mobile Veterinary Section to report on use, expending. Air N. Co. No. 16 inspected later by DDVS 2 Army. a/	
30-12-15	Visited 43 Infantry Brigade Area & inspected all 15 Transport animals. Sore ones said to exhibit one dead and three sick. History of injury & sinking so frame or laceration of flint - no evidence of shelter from shoulder - from history it is probably that the Scabies was caused by the corroding of 15 Tons of water biscuit to the armourers of officers, i.e. men & change of hay a diet of Allied air heels. Also the one history here at officers stables to air heels of heavy Carthorse of V.O's. Personnel of the R.V. return. a/	
31.12.15	3 Mobile Vety Section inspected 40 Cases from 2nd Division, and 10 Cases of 4th Fraction a/	

A.D.Y.S.
24th.
vol 5.

Tau

<u>Confidential.</u>

WAR DIARY of

A.D.V.S. 24ᵗʰ DIVISION.

From 1·1·16 To 31·1·16.

Volume (5)

WAR DIARY or INTELLIGENCE SUMMARY.

ADVS 24 Division

Army Form C. 2118.

Hour, Date, Place	Summary of Events and Information	Remarks and References to Appendices
TILQUES 2-1-16	Visited Transport of 9 Norfolk and 13th Middlesex Regts. No 9791 Temp. Sergt W. Brown, ACC lately attached to 107 Brigade R.F.A. Reprimanded, attached to 36 Mobile Veterinary Section for observation and report recorded to his permanent rank for Inefficiency under the conditions of Annex 302 & 303 K.R. — DDVS 3rd Army V/792 dated 31-12-15. ob.	
" 3-1-16	DDVS 2nd Army called. Inspected chief suspected Mange from back Horses Brigade R.F.A. (51st) — Arranged for isolation on a unit from S Omer Station. et	
" 4-1-16	Visited Transports. Three Field Companies RE. while on march— Sent for cases Itchin disease from 19th Company ASC and 72 field Ambulance to 36. Mobile Veterinary Section. 39 Animals from 9th Division and 17th Tractors evacuated by 36 Mobile Veterinary Section. ob	
" 5-1-16	Informed ADVS 9 Division of number Tractors by Itchina (?) — Who were visited by OC 36. Mobile Veterinary Section and wrote	

Army Form C. 2118.

WAR DIARY
or
INTELLIGENCE SUMMARY.
(Erase heading not required.)

Instructions regarding War Diaries and Intelligence
Summaries are contained in F. S. Regs., Part II.
and the Staff Manual respectively. Title pages
will be prepared in manuscript.

Hour, Date, Place	Summary of Events and Information	Remarks and References to Appendices
TILQUES. 5-1-16 (cont'd)	Wrote	
" 6-1-16	to Farrier at	
	3rd Mobile Veterinary Section left for ARNEKE en route to Renescure the three left in Section billets arranged for their	
	takenover by 29 Mobile Veterinary Section at	
TILQUES. 7-1-16	3rd Mobile Veterinary Section evacuated 11 animals 1st ARNEKE at	
STEENVOORDE " P.M.	left TILQUES with Divisional H.Q. and arrived STEENVOORDE at	
RENINGHELST. 8-1-16	Arrived RENINGHELST opened office at 12.30 p.m.	
	visited major lines of 2nd Divisional Train. Signal Company R.E.	
	and 36 Mobile Veterinary Section.	
" 9-1-16	Interview with O.C. Division. Had following needed in Divisional	
	Order - "complete" Checked that all accidents to be reported because of	
	sufficiency animal losses and mules while in this area. It is a	
	precautionary measure to hold spare animals which will	
	suffer with duffin." at	
" 10-1-16	Visited 2nd D.A.C. Theorem of horses and my het let	
	much X evidence, reported matter to O.C. 2nd D.A.C. at	
	Reed Lund A.V.C. provisional ordnans on horse in England. 10.6.17 inst.	

Form/C. 2118/11.

Army Form C. 2118.

WAR DIARY
or
INTELLIGENCE SUMMARY.
(Erase heading not required.)

Hour, Date, Place	Summary of Events and Information	Remarks and references to Appendices
PENINGHURST. 11-1-16	DDVS. 2nd Army gave a demonstration at No 36. Mobile Veterinary Section n to Inter divnal Vetynal Meets Mullewington. reports abt Ancre trench r Nervin at	
" 12-1-16	Lt Pulley. ave. VO% to H.B. R.G.A reported at his office. Under instructions from DDVS. 2 Army - visited ADVS. 2nd Canadian Division. Saw a be actg to Mallein (inter divnal helpontal Matters). Visited 3b M.VS. & 197 Company A.S.C. at	
" 13-1-16	Visited Wagon lines of 19. 72. 73 I.D. Stationary Arnet. (at approaches taken to mak Trough very muddy. Took in draft programme of Mallein testing 7 division to A.A.D.M.G. 22 than. 36 M.V Section Mallein at	
" 14.1.16	Prepare programme of Mallering Animals of the division in Consultation with O Brand, CRA. CRE. applied VO's parrangement made.	

WAR DIARY
or
INTELLIGENCE SUMMARY.
(Erase heading not required.)

Army Form C. 2118.

Hour, Date, Place	Summary of Events and Information	Remarks and references to Appendices
RENINGHELST. 14.1.16 (a.m.)	Conference of V.O.'s. Reprehn. of M.ch. Returns. Lt. M. Pilkey A.V.C. attached 11" Heavy Brigade R.G.A. attached to Division. 4 Horses. 3 B.M.V. Section Mallievres. 36 Mobile Veterinary Section evacuated 31 animals, 20 Division and 8 I.O.L. Inverbal.	
" 15.1.16	D.D.V.S. – 2nd Army called & left spare parts for Syringes. at. Visited 30th V.S. Saw animals that had been mallienes. at Sch. Home. Glasgow Yeomany mallienes. at	
" 16.1.16	Visited Glasgow Yeomany saw animals Taken – also 2nd D.A.C. and 106 Brigade A.C. R.F.A. Interview T.G. O.C. showed results of sick horse when attention to hand – with highest percentages. One G.O.C. previlige Meeting In 2nd Army for Barats, had also notes by hints for December. Stan G. O.C. memo, reference Postponed of M. Vet. Section 17th Corps Troops – R.V.C. do not express approval. Total 2 Horses & 8 Mules. at	

WAR DIARY
INTELLIGENCE SUMMARY

Army Form C. 2118.

Hour, Date, Place	Summary of Events and Information	Remarks and references to Appendices
RENINGHELST. 17-1-16	Visited animals lines at 74 Field Ambulance. Strength Table :- 72 Field Ambulance Officers 8 Men 220 " 73 " " 10 " 210 " 74 " " 10 " 217 Glasgow Yeomanry 10 " oh/	
" 18-1-16	Visited units. Returned as 17" ind. & found all correct. 73 Field Ambulance - 28 thro' - 2 Mile Isolated. No 7637 Cpoul ANDERSON.J. A.V.C. Cld to A.D.M.S. of Division, admitted sick - Disease CORYZA. Strength Isolated:- 74 Field Ambulance Mile 2. 72 " " " 14. ch/	
" 19-1-16	Visited cases of multiple m-rash in whole 973 Field Ambulance. Some had Rothug. Three Pimple. Organisation to hoppor be slight Problem at present. Old re those smelling ins. Sept Ministry. Kenee ins list ran employer on This exp. Strength Isolated. 73 Field Ambulance. Horse 2.	

WAR DIARY
or
INTELLIGENCE SUMMARY.
(Erase heading not required.)

Army Form C. 2118.

Hour, Date, Place	Summary of Events and Information	Remarks and references to Appendices

RENINGHELST. 19-1-16 (Cont'd). Animal Total - 194 Coy ASC. Horse. 61.
              92 Field Ambulance " 2. Mules 10.

20.1.16

17'Infantry Brigade.
        Horses Mules
8/Buffs.   23. 43
12/Royal Fusiliers 32 30
1st/Royal Fusiliers 57 — do

Tested - 195 Company A.S.C. 77 Horses. Mule hill
" 72 I.B. { 1/N. Stafford 52 - 4
      8/W. Kents 24 - 38
" 73 I.B. { 2/Leinsters 39 - —
      4/Northants 12 - 36 do

Visits arrived of 2nd Divisional Cyclists.

21.1.16

Tested - 194 Company ASC - 54 Horses.
" Details at D.H.Q. 68 "
2/Londons 57
3/Rifle Brigade 54.

WAR DIARY
INTELLIGENCE SUMMARY
(Erase heading not required.)

Army Form C. 2118.

Hour, Date, Place	Summary of Events and Information	Remarks and references to Appendices
RENINGHELST 21.1.16 (Cont'd)	Total - 9/East Surreys — Men 93 Mules 39	
	7th 8/Queens " 23 " 32	
	Mounted 8/Middlesex " 2nd " 40 1	
	Brigade V.Bns. " 3 " 10	
	93 Infantry { 9/Lincolns " 20	
	Brigade 9/N.Lancs " 11 2/	
	Total 196 Company R.E. " 43	
	73 Infantry { 13/Middlesex " 11 33	
	Brigade 9/R.Sussex " 8 35	
	H.Bns. " 11 10	
	14 Infantry Brigade H.Qrs. " 28	
	Reports 9/East Surreys and 9/R.Sussex Reg't for not complying	
	with D.R.O. No.26. advice 9-1-16 (Putting depth to the link	
	of arrival to prevent item breaking)	
23-1-16	Total:- D.H.Q. 28 Mound - Mules —	
	R.E. Signal Company 56 - 7	

WAR DIARY
or
INTELLIGENCE SUMMARY.

(Erase heading not required.)

Army Form C. 2118.

Hour, Date, Place	Summary of Events and Information	Remarks and references to Appendices
RENINGHELST. 23-1-16	(Cont'd) Tested :— 194 Company ASC. 39 Horses	
	⎰ 19b Company ASC ⎱	
	⎱ 13/Middlesex ⎰ 17	
	73 ⎰ 9/R.Sussex 19	
	Infantry ⎱ HQ 73 Infantry Brigade 4	
	Brigade	
	Tested Signal Company R.E. 18 + CRE 2 Horses	
	197 Company ASC. 80. 194 Coy ASC 16 "	
24-1-16	17 Infantry Brigade M.G. Section 40 Horses 2 Mules all	
	Visited 24 D.A.C. being Veterinary Officer reported that the	
	Condition of some Sections the Small Section (?) of No I - good condition;	
	Ammunition Section, fair. No 2 Section - poor, showing condition. No 3	
	Section, fair but there is noticeable loss of condition. Standing of	
	Section 2 & 3 Gnd - hard frost hard, including dry harness.	
25-1-16	Mr arranged line for to have logs & Marguerite racks - Remover	
	the Feed of feeding & weights Civilian feeds (sour) correct. Only	
	air passed Hay inner, but Oat-etting is also inner when	
	procurable.	

WAR DIARY
INTELLIGENCE SUMMARY

Army Form C. 2118.

Hour, Date, Place	Summary of Events and Information	Remarks and references to Appendices
RENINGHELST 25.1.16 (cont)	Proceeded.	
26-1-16	Inoculated Horses for Anthrax, those reported to be infected & not diseased. Stop taken. New stable-up will be provided & not disinfected.	
	Tested - 2nd D.A.C. 137 horses. 64 Mules. Bri's. Cyclist 1 Horse 2 Mules	
	12 Infantry Brig H.Q. 19 " 4 " 8/Queens 7 " — ah	
	9/ South Staffords 3 "	
	Tested 103/F Coy R.E. 43 " 28 " 104/F Coy RE 42 " 36 " ah	
	107 Bde R.F.A. 137 "	
27-1-16	108 Bde R.F.A. 144 3rd D.A.C. 32 horses	
	2 Sec/ D.A.C. 15-8 " 46 Mules 129 F Coy R.E. 42 " 29 Mules	
	163/F Coy R.E. 12 " 107 Bde R.F.A. 84 "	
	Report received from HAZEBROUCK that No 6105 Pte Prior G.F. A/C. 36 Mobile Veterinary Section arrested for Drunkenness.	
	Escort dispatched to take over accused. at	
28-1-16	Tried No 6105 Pte Prior R.G.F. A.V.C. remanded for F.G.C.M.	
	Tested 105 Bde R.F.A. 284 Horses 32 Mules.	
	Weekly Expenses Veterinary Officers. ah	

Army Form C. 2118.

WAR DIARY
or
INTELLIGENCE SUMMARY.
(Erase heading not required.)

Hour, Date, Place	Summary of Events and Information	Remarks and references to Appendices
RENINGHELST 29-1-16	Held interview with 9 O.C. Divisian Mobile discussed Crisis standing work of our D.A.S. Sick horses: Unit failing to comply with routine Orders regarding animal management prevention of disease and injuries to animals. Totals 3rd Sec D.V.C. 161 Horses. 37 Mules. 108 Bde R.F.A. 108 " 107 Bde R.F.A. 107 Horses 12/Sherwood Foresters 25 " 65 Mules	
30-1-16	Visited A.D.V.S. 2 Canadian Division from whose lines at but had re-acted to intra dermal preparal method of Mallein test: new method of hypodermic mallein in side of neck. Lieut T/Sherwood Foresters 12 Horses. 109 Brigade R. F.A. 111 " S/Sgt No 12663 L/Cpl ROGERS. E.W. A.V.C. Clerk to A.D.V.S. arrived.	
" 31-1-16	Relief of Cpl ANDERSON A.V.C. escorted sick. at tested 109 Brigade R.F.A. 6 Horses. 67 Mules.	

(9 29 6) W 2794 100,000 8/14 H W V Forms/C. 2118/11.

Army Form C. 2118.

WAR DIARY
or
INTELLIGENCE SUMMARY.
(Erase heading not required.)

Instructions regarding War Diaries and Intelligence Summaries are contained in F. S. Regs., Part II. and the Staff Manual respectively. Title pages will be prepared in manuscript.

Hour, Date, Place	Summary of Events and Information	Remarks and references to Appendices
RENINGHELST. 31-1-16 (cont)	Tested 108 Brigade R.F.A. 122 Horses ad 109 " " " " 161 " " "	

A.D.B. 24th Div.
Vol: 6

Confidential

WAR DIARY of

ADVS. 24ᵗʰ Division

From 1.2.16 to 29.2.16

Volume (6)

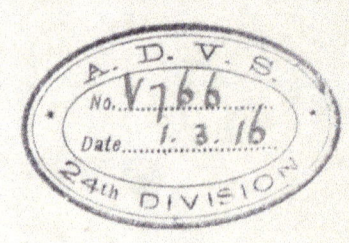

WAR DIARY
or
INTELLIGENCE SUMMARY

ADVS. 24th DIVISION.

Army Form C. 2118.

(Erase heading not required.)

Hour, Date, Place	Summary of Events and Information	Remarks and references to Appendices
RENINGHELST. 1.2.16	G.O.C. Division ruled that S.E. No 6105. Pte PRIOR G.F. AVC. No 3rd Mobile Veterinary Section should be dealt with by ADVS. Charge- "Disobeying a lawful command given him by his superior Officer, and "Drunkenness". Awarded 28 days Field Punishment- No I. Total 108 Brigade R.F.A. 111 Horses.	
" 2.2.16	DDVS 2nd Army called reference bulletin listing of division. a/y Visited B/108 Brigade R.F.A. to see a dratipt [draught?] hunter. Occurred in agreement that joined on or about 9th Jan'y 1916. No/ 31/16.— Near Sgt. 2d" hunter. Lame his Shoulder. tense — Painful. — Painful discharge inner canthus — Conjunctiva inflamed — Temperature 102.4. Officer's (inoculated 1.7.16) seen by me this morning — knee his swollen. tense & painful. hyper [?] id slightly swollen. Purulent discharge from inner canthus — Conjunctiva highly inflamed. The Veterinary Officer did not report any swelling of upper lid from eye.	

Form/C.2118/11

WAR DIARY
INTELLIGENCE SUMMARY
(Erase heading not required.)

Army Form C. 2118.

Hour, Date, Place	Summary of Events and Information	Remarks and references to Appendices

RENINGHELST. 2.2.16 (Cont'd) — J.nos Lorries slight snow at 4 & 8 hours. Arrival very dull. Horse Report to D.D.V.S. 2 Army recommended destruction as animal had vexated.

Total Horses R.P.A. 1057/Horses. 3 Mules
" " " 167 " 112 "
" " " 108 " 59 " 25 "

36 M.V.S. inspected – 28 Sick Animals – 5 Cases to Rest Farms, and 8 Cases evac. to 6 Vety Van Kilwinning returned.

3.2.16 — Received orders from D.D.V.S. 2 Army – V.786. d/2/2/16 (Telegram) to destroy mule mule R.N.8. Proceeded to the kraal. destroyed horse made P.N.8. I also made an H.Li – medium examination as follows:—Near eye at 72' Horse Swelling of upper and lower lids but no apparent and purulent discharge from inner canthus had subsided.

WAR DIARY
INTELLIGENCE SUMMARY
(Erase heading not required.)

Army Form C. 2118.

Hour, Date, Place	Summary of Events and Information	Remarks and references to Appendices
RENINGHELST. 3.2.16 (Cont'd)	Sick visited. Office at No 8 Howe. Here was a horse and foot Shelling here painful. Animal very dull. Post-mortem examination — Nasal septum, larynx, and trachea apparently normal. Lungs — a severe nodular front in upper third of right lung. There were one or two haemorrhagic areas in right lung. Spleen a nodular body not found, situated just beneath the capsule at Republic attached to Q branch and CRA, 11 Div Artillery.	
4.2.16.	Health Conference Veterinary Officers. Visited 120 Howitzer Brigade R.F.A. at 107	
5.2.16	D.D.V.S. 2 Army called reference supply of Calcium Sulphide Stations. Interview with OC Division reference sick horses. Month of January	
6.2.16	Tested 19 horses of 108 Brigade R.F.A. Visited 73 Field Ambulance. 36 Mules.	

Forms/C. 2118/11

WAR DIARY
or
INTELLIGENCE SUMMARY.
(Erase heading not required.)

Army Form C. 2118.

Hour, Date, Place	Summary of Events and Information	Remarks and references to Appendices
RENINGHELST 7-2-16	Tested 109 Brigade R.F.A. B.2 Horses. Visited 2nd D.A.C. Exercise had caused 7 colic (resulting in death) several animals. The pulling harness was deficient:— 1) Supply of harness inspection. Sometimes two days elapse before any is issued. 2) Irregular hours, for too late before arr. There is a great deal of night work. 3) Method of feeding grain not properly mixed with chaff given. The water too good. Improperly given + animal affected had no history of liability to colic. No one the oil + linseed mixed — smoked. Recommended — 1) Thorough change of manger + wagner. 2) feeds from box a day. 3) less chaff. 4) Ah feeds to be held in nose bags. 5) Clover hay. Should also be held mixed with molasses. Try again in a week. 6) sick animal 1½ – 2 hour before work. Referred to D.R.A. + O.C. D.A.C. at	

WAR DIARY or INTELLIGENCE SUMMARY

Army Form C. 2118.

Hour, Date, Place	Summary of Events and Information	Remarks and references to Appendices
RENINGHELST. 8.2.16	Visited 36th Mobile Veterinary Section. horses inspection to ascertain the section render on all sign boards, & the Divisional sign. Permission obtained from D.D.V.S. 2nd Army to visit Veterinary hospitals at the Base. Among Conveyance with 2/16 accompany A.D.V.S. 2nd Canadian Division. at.	
" 9.2.16 p.m.	Proceed with A.D.V.S. 2nd Canadian Division to Boulogne.	
BOULOGNE 10.2.16	Visited 13 Veterinary Hospital. Saw sick later from train on arrival, method of checking, sorting & distribution to the hospitals. also visited No 3, 10, & 12 Veterinary Hospitals. See Pamphlet on "The Co-divisible working of a Vety Hospital".	
RENINGHELST. 11.2.16	Returned RENINGHELST. Conference of Veterinary Officer in afternoon. Report M F A 2000.	
" 12.2.16.	Visited 108 Bde R.F.A. veterinary Sergt Hill A.V.C. at D Battery. hearth interview with O.C. Division. Sept. Donohy A.V.C. at 17th Infantry Brigade encamped sick on 11.2.16. at	

Army Form C. 2118.

WAR DIARY
or
INTELLIGENCE SUMMARY.
(Erase heading not required.)

Instructions regarding War Diaries and Intelligence Summaries are contained in F. S. Regs., Part II. and the Staff Manual respectively. Title pages will be prepared in manuscript.

Hour, Date, Place	Summary of Events and Information	Remarks and references to Appendices
RENINGHELST. 13.2.16	Visited 36 A.V.S. Saw For Sergeant A.V.C. in connection with signing of indentation of Veternary tins. expires Section D new. RL	
" 14.2.16	Went to division Stopped lorry to enquiries in YPRES SECTOR. Visited 36 M.S. section evacuating at	
" 15.2.16	36 hrs evacuated 36 animals from the division and 5 from the Formation. Total 185 Mules. 91 O.B.W. R. ga.	
	1 Mule (death the re-action) 873 Field Ambulance. Issued instructions re clipping of Mules. Veterinary Cont. at Proceeded Without delay to Appleton and Boardman. A.V.C.	
" 17.2.16	36 hrs L: AVC Base Records for verification of dates of inoculation. Lectured with Mallein- 3 Horses of H.Q. R.A. a.b.	
" 18.2.16	Lt MacGregor proceeded on leave to United Kingdom from 18-28 February 1916.	

WAR DIARY
or
INTELLIGENCE SUMMARY.
(Erase heading not required.)

Army Form C. 2118.

Hour, Date, Place	Summary of Events and Information	Remarks and references to Appendices
RENINGHELST. 18.2.16 (Cont'd)	Issued electric torches to Veterinary Officers.	
" 19.2.16	Weekly conference preliminary officers preparation of A.T. A 2000.	
" 20.2.16	Weekly report to G.O.C. Division. Visited 30 H.S. and saw cascade destruction 107 sick P. Heads at	
" 21.2.16	Visited 73 Field Ambulance.	
" 23.2.16	Visited 36 H.S. Slaughter for art animals completed at	
	36 H/S evacuated 20 animals of this division and 3 of other divisions. at	
" 24.2.16	Visited 106 Brigade R.F.A. at	
" 25.2.16	Veterinary Officers weekly conference & preparation of weekly return.	
" 26.2.16	Air raid on RENINGHELST. 3 mules killed in field with 100 yards of office, 4 ponts. heavily injured with G.O.C. Division. h stoning him himself casualty action, to remarks that the Capt. who dies of actual military casualties. Shot in animals	

WAR DIARY
or
INTELLIGENCE SUMMARY.
(Erase heading not required.)

Army Form C. 2118.

Hour, Date, Place	Summary of Events and Information	Remarks and references to Appendices
RENINGHELST 26.2.16 (Cont'd)	Arrivals	
	Killed by shell fire while asleep in billet and Died.	
	He arrived from hops lines and appeared to be in fine a	
	certain number of deaths from his own men recently.	
28.2.16	Visited 36 while Infirmary Section van car for evacuation.	
	Also the cases admitted for paraplegia from 72" Infantry	
	Brigade. He enquired of paraplegia & O.C. who spoke that	
	did not show any signs on admittance - case will be returned	
	to duty. Visited 72" Infantry Brigade.	
	Trieh Thrusch hose depensaving. Lamps defective - will be retired	
	when lamp is in use. ad	
29.2.16	Visited 107 Brigade R.F.A. and 36 M.O. ad	

Confidential

War Diary of

A.D.V.S. 24th Division.

From 1.3.16 To 31.3.16

Volume (7).

WAR DIARY
or
INTELLIGENCE SUMMARY. ADVS 24th DIVISION

Army Form C. 2118.

(Erase heading not required.)

Hour, Date, Place	Summary of Events and Information	Remarks and references to Appendices
RENINGHELST. 1.3.16	36 Mobile Veterinary Section evacuated 31 from his division and received from another Formation. Visited DADOS and held a returned Thornton Forge Apparatus which was found to be in working order.	
" 2.3.16	Visited 108 Brigade R.H. & D. Battery animals poor looking. Suspension in wagon lines. Hock & hog tenure nets not returned. Standings not good. Offered approaches bad. Made personal report to CRA. DDVS 2nd Army called at Office requiring Sergeants AVC instructed to proceed when animals are examined. ay left behind. Visited 109 Brigade R.F.A.	
" 3.3.16	Weekly conference Veterinary Officers. Gave demonstration to them on Thornton Forge. Inspected weekly returns. Eight deaths from Abdominal trouble probably due to irregular feeding intervals caused Whizzling situation influenced by inclement weather, ah	

WAR DIARY
or
INTELLIGENCE SUMMARY
(Erase heading not required.)

Army Form C. 2118.

Instructions regarding War Diaries and Intelligence Summaries are contained in F. S. Regs., Part II. and the Staff Manual respectively. Title pages will be prepared in manuscript.

Hour, Date, Place		Summary of Events and Information	Remarks and references to Appendices
RENINGHELST	4.3.16	Hourly interviews with 9. O.C. Division. Visited 11 Heavy Brigade R.G.A. ab/	
"	5.3.16	Visited 93 Field Ambulance. ab/	
"	6.3.16	Visited Mr Sam Cases for attention & evacuation. ab/	
"	8.3.16	Lt. W.A. MACGREGOR A.V.C. reported sick. Strains Oxyza. Probable duration 3 days. 43 Cases evacuated from this division or one 17 Division. Showers of rain in due to inclement weather and bad weather. Visited 3 h.r.s. ab/	
"	9.3.16	Visited Fleming Knoll. 1 Brigade R.F.A. 106 Battalion 34 B.A.C. Glasgow Yeomanry and 7 Field Ambulance. Made temporary (in the returning attendance on himself) M. Macgregor. Lt. L.A. LEACH A.V.C. 106 Brigade returned from leave should have reported by the 7th inst. ab/	
"	10.3.16	Hourly conference. Veterinary Officers. Preparation of A.F.A. 2000. Owing to the present inclement weather the number of	

Army Form C. 2118.

WAR DIARY
or
INTELLIGENCE SUMMARY.
(Erase heading not required.)

Instructions regarding War Diaries and Intelligence Summaries are contained in F. S. Regs., Part II. and the Staff Manual respectively. Title pages will be prepared in manuscript.

Hour, Date, Place	Summary of Events and Information	Remarks and references to Appendices
RENING-HELST 10.3.16 (Cont'd)	Cases of mumps, measles & nevers. Some standing here awaiting men will be procured at	
11.3.16	Visited men in line M.Y. Spruth, Brigade, 142 Field Ambulance at	
12.3.16	Reed; W. B. Torell. A.V.C. (T.C.) arrived. Replace Revd L. H. LEACH, A.V.C. (T.C.) on leave on medical certificate. at had chy interview with D. D. V. S. Division	
March 3rd		
13.3.16	Visited 109 Brigade R.F.A. wagon lines — also 36 M.S. D D V S 2nd Army called. 72nd and 73rd Infantry Brigade Machine Gun Companies arrived from ENGLAND. Sleigh French in Horses q. Mules 4.2.	
14.3.16	Visited Divisional Train and 73rd Infantry Brigade Major Lines at	
15.3.16	Visited 72 & 73 Companies, Machine Gun Corps, men arrived from England. Found myself to veterinary stores only, one Sanitaker Company v no men under training. Visited 36 M.S. Reported for duty to Lieut: H.D. Shaw to walk-early at	
16.3.16	Visited Jn. D.A.C. No 2 Section here transtanding at	

WAR DIARY
or
INTELLIGENCE SUMMARY.

(Erase heading not required.)

Hour, Date, Place	Summary of Events and Information	Remarks and references to Appendices
Reninghelst. 17.3.16	36 h.v.S. executed 25 animals. Two Ambulances arrived. heavy expense of Veterinary Officer. Preparation of travel reports. Reported A.P.M. and Officer Commanding Wilton driving & hitting H.D. Horse in neck — seems to think not. The two for galloping acts — at a the Park. Commenced new Division to 3rd Canadian Divisional area.	
" 18.3.16	Visited FLÊTRE and 3rd Canadian Mule Watering Section. Arranged Watering on later of 21st inst. D.D.V.S. 2nd Army Corps & visited 36 h.v.S. with him & saw the Ambulance rates discussed the move of F. Division Mule horse areas. half interview with G. O.C. Division. Queen obtain Trumpets of Pick-up Mule Injuries. AA & QMQ Carriage Inspection of artillery horses by an Officer horse & harness Cavalry left attch. at	

WAR DIARY
or
INTELLIGENCE SUMMARY.
(Erase heading not required.)

Army Form C. 2118.

Hour, Date, Place	Summary of Events and Information	Remarks and references to Appendices
RENINGHELST. 19.3.16	Visited 3rd Canadian Division hqrs lines, and D.H.Q. 1st Canadian Division at St Jans Cappel. Visited 36 MVS & moved mules to proceed to Le Coq de Paille or Tuesday 21st inst and took on 3rd Canadian MVS billet. Sent Trenton Spaniels to new area K.V.O's with R.F.A. Brigades — Men to report personally at this office on 24th inst at FLÊTRE. al	
" 21.3.16	Left RENINGHELST 9.30 a.m. Arrived FLÊTRE 10.30 a.m. Reported arrival & N.I. of 36 MVS in new area to DDVS. 2nd Army. of	
FLÊTRE "		
" 22.3.16	Visited hqrs lines of 73rd Infantry Brigade at ———— Two officers walked arrived.	
" 23.3.16	DDVS— 2nd Army called A.M. Visited R.F.A. area. Found two horses of latter DAC left at camp on received by 2nd DAC. One man 21 years service. Nervous & very emaciated was destroyed. Also a case of P.V.N. Visited by 36 MVS. Visited hqrs lines of 9th East Surrey Regt. Left officers wallet for Capt Blackburn. A.V. d 107 Br R.F.A. I.Q. ok	

WAR DIARY
or
INTELLIGENCE SUMMARY

(Erase heading not required.)

Army Form C. 2118.

Hour, Date, Place	Summary of Events and Information	Remarks and references to Appendices
FLÊTRE 24.3.16	Visited Hq, Lutow, Befr R.S. at CAESTRE, and 36 M.V.S. also 104 Field Company R.E. Found Starkey my representative regulated Same, at horses experience F.V.O.'s at	
" 25.3.16	Visited C.R.E. and 73 Field Ambulance at EECKE, and 17 Infantry Brigade. DDVS 2nd Army were inspecting the Horses Chine eyesore & left 3 for the use of the division in charge of A.D.V.S. had y intervien with G.O.C. Division. at	
" 26.3.16	Visited Machine Gun Companies.	
" 27.3.16	San Marsahg reference the issue of field forge to R.F.A. units to a number of shoes got broken during process of setting and fitting. Visited Sr JANS CAPPEL and San ADVS 1st Canadian Division reference more of the Mobile Veterinary Section. At present the 1st Canadian MVS doesn't move until 1st April. Visited Sr Sylvestre Cappel and inspected these 4 Mules 61 being Trans Jerred from this division & Sm Base Transport. Animals proceeding by road to ABBEVILLE.	

WAR DIARY
INTELLIGENCE SUMMARY

Army Form C. 2118.

Hour, Date, Place	Summary of Events and Information	Remarks and references to Appendices
FLÊTRE 27.3.16 (cont'd)	Units only had afternoon notice to prepare to march. We here free from contagious and infectious disease & certificate given to that effect. The shoeing all round was indifferent. Some had turned shoes, others no spare feet required removing and shoeing. The animals in most instances quick-girthed. At the defects now being adjusted by a Shoeing Smith, + a Saddler, sick horses to prevent the gear being matched. Units no veterinary stores for use on the march. At Visited 3rd Rifle Brigade. O'Shea Inn Fraelens. 104 Field Coy; R.E. and 36 M.V.S selected animals for inoculation. At	
" 28.3.16	Visited 107 Bar. T.A. and saw sick animals evacuated at GODAWAERSVELDE Station. 36 M.V.S inoculated hive sick animals of This division, and six of the animals at Armyd with HATS. 2nd Canadian Divison Reserve Veterinary Officers in area until the Divisonal Artillery move.	
" 29.3.16		
" 30.3.16		

Army Form C. 2118.

WAR DIARY
or
INTELLIGENCE SUMMARY.
(Erase heading not required.)

Hour, Date, Place	Summary of Events and Information	Remarks and references to Appendices
FLÊTRE 30.3.16 (cont'd)	Left list plans left to Veen with HDVS - 1st Canadian Brain. Reported arrival to DDVS- 2nd Army and Signals.	
S.t JANS CAPPEL 30.3.16	Left FLÊTRE 9.15.a.m en route S.t Jans Cappel 9.45 a.m. Visited 1st Canadian Mobile Veterinary Section on the BAILLEUL - NIEPPE Road.	at
" 31.3.16	Visited units of 72" & 71" Canadian Brigades, 196 Company A.S.C. and 7th Field Ambulance. Asked for has been sent attack of 1st North Staffords. This unit had no deaths from Rupture practices. Reported to DDVS- 2nd Army and O'Brien. Held conference of Veterinary Officers + preparation of A.F. A2000.	at

ADVS 24 Div Vol 8

CONFIDENTIAL

War Diary of

ADVS. 24ᵗʰ Division

From. 1.4.16   To. 30.4.16

Volume (8)

WAR DIARY ADVS. 24th DIVISION. Army Form C. 2118.

or

INTELLIGENCE SUMMARY.

(Erase heading not required.)

Hour, Date, Place	Summary of Events and Information	Remarks and references to Appendices
St Jans Cappel 1-4-16	Visited 36th I.S. remained for Capt. J.H. Laurie, A.V.C. to answer for me during my absence on leave.	
" 2-4-16	Interview with G.O.C. Division, reported to him doing of special work. One matter given to me Lect'a. & hurler asked I take pack to Division Orders rale intr-married at	
	Proceed to Boulogne en route to England on leave. Capt. J.H. Laurie. A.V.C. taking over duties of ADVS during my absence. at	
" 3. 4. 16	No 662 Sergeant BOARDMAN, J. A.V.C. signed A.F.W.3125 and proceed same day on leave for the north to PARIS, Special permission having been obtained from I Corps. at	
" 11. 4. 16	Returned Paris from leave. at	
" 12.4.16	Lt. T.F. HOLCHRIS A.V.C. evacuated sick to Base-replaced same by No 17DDVS. 2d Army, & relieved D.H.Q. Visited I Corps Headquarters. at	
" 13.4.16	Visited 24th D.A.C. Man demobilities 7 Thornton Field Forge as the	

Forms/C. 2118/11

Army Form C. 2118.

WAR DIARY
or
INTELLIGENCE SUMMARY.
(Erase heading not required.)

Instructions regarding War Diaries and Intelligence Summaries are contained in F. S. Regs., Part II. and the Staff Manual respectively. Title pages will be prepared in manuscript.

Hour, Date, Place	Summary of Events and Information	Remarks and references to Appendices
S¹ Jans Cappel. 13.4.16 (cont)	a.m. O.C. 2nd D.A.C. has reported informally on the Horses when 3 down. Telemps. Found the pumps defective & water too contaminated. His most instruction which he obtained N.C.O., who agrees, has admitted of promotion upnt. Inspected all the animals of 2nd D.A.C. with D.D.R. 2ⁿᵈ Army. The Section (No. 2) has been worried from telephone experience & its Camp in from area, but am informing him later. Young horses were evacuated for a Rest Farm. Hereby Conference Veterinary Officers & preparation of meeting returns.	
" 14.4.16	at	
" 15.4.16	Visited 36 A.V.S. M Lestre Bach R.8 16 Siege Company R.M. R.8. Captain F.W. Trydell MC arrived. hurth interview with G.O.C. Division, at	
" 16.4.16	Visited 109 Brigade R.F.A. at	
" 17.4.16	Visited Bailleul to look for a billet as office. Capt. Trydell AVC called & gave him instructions re med return etc. etc.	

WAR DIARY
~~INTELLIGENCE~~ SUMMARY
(Erase heading not required.)

Army Form C. 2118.

Hour, Date, Place	Summary of Events and Information	Remarks and references to Appendices
S⁺ Jans Cappel 18.4.16 Bailleul	Left S⁺ Jans Cappel at 9 a.m. Arrived Bailleul at 9.20 a.m. and opened office. 21 Mules and 9 Horses of the 72nd Infantry Brigade Machine Gun Company visited by the Veterinary Officer polished Métier. Visited The Company gave recommendation as regards finding same of oral hay hay nets. The latter were not being used. The one Shoeing-Smith is sick so made arrangements for Shoeing to be done by Armament Mounted unit (10th Bn. D.C.O.) The new Shoeing-Smith is training as a Shoeing-Smith. Officers Company sent for training as a Shoeing-Smith. 23 Mules of 73rd Machine Gun Company holsters.	
" 19.4.16	Visited 142 Bn. R.G.A met Lt. Howard R.V.C. Sept. Madras R.V.C. officer Battery has applied for Lt. Howard for attendance on Influenza him said he moved here transferred stable in interest in his duties. Visited 72nd Machine Gun Company horses of polishering. Visited 73 " " " " " " front At H.Q. I line a Transport officer - the supervision here horse Top will help now being used, animals too crowded.	

WAR DIARY or INTELLIGENCE SUMMARY

Army Form C. 2118.

Hour, Date, Place	Summary of Events and Information	Remarks and references to Appendices
BAILLEUL 19.4.16 (Cont'd)	Crowded.	
20.4.16	Report to Q Divisional Headquarters at Visited the section 4/7 D.A.C. Horses of II Corps H.Q. Tried to interview Falphebal vet of Br Mules, 72" Machine Gun Company. Mules 19. Horses 9 of 73rd Machine Gun Company. Went to Bailleul Station to see 11 Remounts found for L.D. Horses of 2nd D.A.C. attached 129 Field Company R.E. making in an unfit condition. Set item that Company with instructions the sent to 36 F. Vet. Section for necessity at _____	
21.4.16	Visited Glasgow Yeomanry & inspected arrivals & returning equipment. They were sent to 36 M.V. Section for examination to ascertain health. Enquiry of veterinary officers. Left the Remounts not sick. Glasgow Yeomanry to use in march if necessary at ____ D.D.V.S. 2nd Army called left spare parts for Hodier syringes. Got more from Tom Major for experience of A.D.V.S.	
22.4.16	Visited 108 Brigade D.Vet.Surg. B.A.Column at ____	
23.4.16	hardly interview with 9 O.C. Division. returned Rest Centre here a	

WAR DIARY
INTELLIGENCE SUMMARY.

Army Form C. 2118.

Hour, Date, Place	Summary of Events and Information	Remarks and references to Appendices
BAILLEUL 23.4.16 (Sun)	Wet, snowy & frosty up to noon, but has been fine in the afternoon. Quite though the gale when the vehicles are on the road. Do particular notice expect relation that troops will ride with their horses not because of feed in winter. at	
" 24.4.16	Visited 2n D.A.C. and 142 H. Batty R.G.A. arranged with V.O for testing lytta which seemed perfectly useful. at	
" 25.4.16	Visited 142 Batty. Visited 70 Hows. Visited 72 Field Ambulance. at	
" 26.4.16	Visited 142 Batty, 8th. Ammn – Visited 77 Hows. 123 HTrMtly R.G.a. lived at from BAILLEUL. Visited 17 D.A.C. found cases of choking from eating cordite husks. at	
" 27.4.16	Capt J.H. IAURIS A.V.C. proceeded on leave from 27/4/16 – 5/5/16. Capt J. Blackham. A.V.C is arranging for him staying at Firth & Seelin. Visit Glasgow Yeomanry sent four temporary lame horses for treatment 63CKN.S. To be sent back T Yeomanry on their return from training with the 2nd Cavalry Division at	
" 28.4.16	Visited C/107 Bde R.F.A reference case of Peripetic Horse.	

WAR DIARY
INTELLIGENCE SUMMARY.
(Erase heading not required.)

Army Form C. 2118.

Hour, Date, Place	Summary of Events and Information	Remarks and references to Appendices
Bailleul 28.4.16 (cont'd)	nil.	
	Succession G.M. & Section officers came and two Sanitarians – two Article's variaties & suites. Division of D.V.S. Co: head no 78 d 21/16. Complied with. Inspection all animals of this unit & found none other suspicious.	
	Health Conference M.O.'s preparation of A.F.A. 2000. Remarks on danger of indicating with trench below the experience index which had examples of this animals in one Command Bunkir.	
	Visited 123 H Battn R.H.A. while in camp on route from unknown destination. Found all animals to being returned well, with cases for r	
	Veterinary equipment in order. at	
29.4.16	Conference at Bailleul of A.D.S.'s - 2 Army. Sanitary Officer II Corps attended. Prink discussed. Disposal of Hos. & New Manure. X.	
	Contamination of water. Disposal of Carcases & vermin. Inspect of camps. Cavacas a risk & contamination of water supply. Visited with Sanitary Officer the manuficture of Bailleul Station. Health Interview with S.O.C. Division. Reported that Animals	

Army Form C. 2118.

WAR DIARY
or
INTELLIGENCE SUMMARY.
(Erase heading not required.)

Hour, Date, Place	Summary of Events and Information	Remarks and references to Appendices
BAILLEUL 29.4.16 (Cont'd)	Animals Staff here in GRAND PLACE - BAILLEUL. I have no arrangements for retaining persons. This fact has been reported to Offr i/c Commanding the Arrivals and orders falling them to bring horse troops they hit to arrange for returning their animals when they are absent from their horse lines at feeding watering times. Also a D. Order has been published to this effect. Shall be in aid of returning in breach recommended troops to terminate at	
30.4.16	Gas attack in our front in effect 9 gas felt in BAILLEUL. Visited all Companies of Divisional Train. Gas effect no slight a number of animals coughed against dust & his nose dull. After ½ hr up in the morning this thin work. Thereafter this the operation there no shelter were not affected at all, while those with shelter were affected as which the still work & Harness were tarnished & leather turned a peculiar colour to simple blanches were used on these animals. Reports have reached me from other units. ad	

SECRET.

WAR DIARY of

A.D.V.S. 24th Division

From 1.5.16 To 31.5.16

Volume (9).

WAR DIARY ADV.S. 24th Division

Army Form C. 2118.

INTELLIGENCE SUMMARY

(Erase heading not required.)

Instructions regarding War Diaries and Intelligence Summaries are contained in F. S. Regs., Part II. and the Staff Manual respectively. Title pages will be prepared in manuscript.

Hour, Date, Place	Summary of Events and Information	Remarks and references to Appendices
BAILLEUL 1-5-16	Visited 3 Un. V.S. & selected animals for evacuation. Accompanied DDR 2nd Army on inspection duty to B.Ruin and Ammunition Column of 108' Brigade R.F.A. A.S.In. - required new horse-rugs. D.B.In. new not using hay-net. Camp of Ammunition Column bad. Standing require repairing. horses having hot Bitumin require more supervision in proper lines, at	
" 2-5-16	Visited heavy H.B. Artillery. Tested 53 Horses. The Care of Sarcoptic Mange in B/106 Brigade R.F.A. Current issued 12ma 1915. Inspect. Mobile Vet. D.vS Githeim 76 Complied with. of	
" 3.5.16	Visited Tom hereabouts at BAILLEUL. Horse lines in hereabouts, as used in Camps. Mules disinfected & disinfected. Inspected animals in BAILLEUL. Visited 74 and 73 field Ambulance camps of Heavy Artillery and 142 H.Bty. R.G.A. of	

Army Form C. 2118.

WAR DIARY
or
INTELLIGENCE SUMMARY.
(Erase heading not required.)

Instructions regarding War Diaries and Intelligence Summaries are contained in F. S. Regs., Part II. and the Staff Manual respectively. Title pages will be prepared in manuscript.

Hour, Date, Place	Summary of Events and Information	Remarks and references to Appendices
BAILLEUL. 4-5-16	Visited B/106 Bde R.F.A. - inspected horses for Skin. Found several officers with lice. Civilian generally poor. Chipping of stables from which affected cases of mange matter. Septic Mange diagnosed microscopically. Animal joined last January. Lot D.D.V.S. 2nd Army at 3/h. & Section. Visited 19th Co. A.S.C. at	
" 5.5.16	Visited 17 D.P.C (Section attached Division) Tested 56 horses 1/1 Mozers H. Batt, R.G.A.	
" 6.5.16	Held conference of V.O. Officers preparation of A.F.A 2000. at Tested 55 horses of 1/1 Wessex H.Bdy. R.G.A. Gave walk repd on Sick Horse Lane L.T.M.R.Sh. § 2nd Division. E.O.C. being absent on leave. at Capt Rawie A.V.C. returned from leave.	
" 7.5.16	Visited D.D.V.S. 2nd Army at HAZEBROUCK in connection with a report by C.R.A that relief since given (this office before Visiting Battery). Visited 72 Field Ambulance. at Visited 107 Bde R.F.A. and 36th Section at	
" 9.5.16		

Army Form C. 2118.

WAR DIARY
or
INTELLIGENCE SUMMARY.
(Erase heading not required.)

Hour, Date, Place	Summary of Events and Information	Remarks and references to Appendices
Bailleul 10.5.16	Visited b/. Siege Battery R.G.A. and 196 Company A.S.C.	
	Blades Cpl. J. Blackburn A.V.C. b visit 167 A.T. Company R.E. at	
" 11.5.16	Visited B/115 Bde R.F.A. enquired its Mule management. This	
	Unit as it is in an unsatisfactory condition. Referred to G.O.C. R.A.	
	Division. Opinion that Mules are neglect generally due to neglect r	
	bad supervision in horse lines.	
	Met D.D.V.S. 2 Army at 38th N. Section – arrangements for fitting spare	
	Slepts to Horse Ambulance.	
	Found 3 horses of 9th D.A.C. attacked to French Mobile Bakery working	
	in harmful condition. Sent them with report T.O.S. 2nd D.A.C. who charges	
	the animals – 3 horses put on sick list. at	
" 12.5.16	Weekly conference Veterinary Officers. Preparation of A.F. A2000.	
	Remarks about inspection forms. Skin Diseases & Rickniends itra	
	bad improve its efficiency. at	
" 13.5.16	Conference T.A.D.'s V.S. 2nd Army at Bailleul.	
	D.D.V.S. 2nd Army Interviews Genl. Robson. 2nd D.A.C. at Bailleul who is	

WAR DIARY
or
INTELLIGENCE SUMMARY.
(Erase heading not required.)

Army Form C. 2118.

Hour, Date, Place	Summary of Events and Information	Remarks and references to Appendices
Bailleul 13.5.16 (Cont'd)	applying for transfer to A.V.C. Major O'Rorke A.V.C. read a paper on "The evacuation of sick animals by road". Discussion re 'Quitor and Horse diseases'. Forwarded report on B/108 Brigade R.F.A. F.A.D.V.S. 2nd Army. Report investigating sick Mules F. Troop and 2/108 & Brigade Train R.B. re Sgt. Artillery. Received notification that the ADVS. 9th Division will resume veterinary administration of II Corps H.Q. Formed Office Capt Shard Heads A.F. H.Doorn & ADVS. 9 Div. & Willfred died. Horses A.V.C. at hostel 3 Fk. 1 Section Heavy Animals have treatment.	
14.5.16	Visit to DAC inspected horses 33. Mules 120. Surplus animals on their organization of Field Artillery Units. Arranged for their treat. and 8 young animals recommended for Cav. Farm — the animals here is four condition exhibit. for issue. Arranged for the supernumerary Sergeants etc. to remain with A. Echelon DAC pending further instructions as to their disposal etc	

WAR DIARY
INTELLIGENCE SUMMARY.

Army Form C. 2118.

Hour, Date, Place	Summary of Events and Information	Remarks and references to Appendices
BAILLEUL 15.5.16	Visited the BAC with DDR/2 Army. Shewed him 20 young horses and 5 Mules but all unconnected to Platform. The remaining Mules, The DDR reminded were in very good condition. These were sent to the Advanced Remount Depot. Visited 36th N. Section and arranged for the section to take over 25 animals at Steenwerck Station.	
" 16.5.16	Proceeded to Steenwerck Station and saw animals trucked for Base. Visited 106 BAC - note No 1. Section 24th BAC - Saw a number of the horses WIL taken on from the DAC. Made suggestions for their improvement. Glasgow Yeomanry & 2nd Dn'l C. which returned from their training with 2nd Cavalry Division at ——	
" 17.5.16	Visited V Corps. Heavy Ammunition Group with VO. VC. hospital. Arrived at Glasgow Yeomanry after return from training. Found on looking fit - in good condition. Visited Abattoir - Bailleul with view to disposing of Australian ewe fit for food.	

WAR DIARY
or
INTELLIGENCE SUMMARY.
(Erase heading not required.)

Army Form C. 2118.

Hour, Date, Place	Summary of Events and Information	Remarks and references to Appendices
BAILLEUL 18.5.16	Visited 3b Mobile Vety Section reported arrivals for evacuation, and treatment in Section. ay	
" 19.5.16	Visited 3/M.V.S in connection with correspondence regarding our Personnel. Held conference of Veterinary Officers and preparation of A.F. H2000. Visited no 4 Section of D.M.C that we moving on 20th inst. Gave times to evacuate by Ambulance. ay	
" 20.5.16	Visited Western Heavy Artillery Battery & Wagon Lemanry. ay	
" 21.5.16	Visited 3b/m V/Section in connection with the fitting spurs. Staff to these Ambulance. Visited D.M.S of New Zealand Artillery. Majority of Horses of The New Zealand and has been to Gallipoli. Are now looking very fit indeed. ay	
" 22.5.16	Visited 3b M V Section selected animals for evacuation. Inspection The animals of new no 4 Section no DMC. Real improvement obtained. Left in condition approving. Visited orchel M DMC attached to 3rd Division II Corps duties. ay	

WAR DIARY
or
INTELLIGENCE SUMMARY.
(Erase heading not required.)

Army Form C. 2118.

Hour, Date, Place	Summary of Events and Information	Remarks and references to Appendices
BAILLEUL. 23.5.16	Visited 73 & 74 Field Ambulance and 142 Bty R.H.A. Inspected animals of & Three attached II Corps H.Qrs.	
" 24.5.16	Spoke to Camp Commandant with reference to supervision of Shoeing Smith Farrier Sergeant who also has the Veterinary work. Sent Farriery & Shoeing Spclts. &c.	
" 25.5.16	Visited 3 M.V. Section &c. Inspected all animals of "D" & "Major" Battery Brigade. Boot improvement in condition. Trotting Stripping, held & application. Withdrawing Shoes in certain cases require attention, particularly in case of preparing hist spreads for Shoes. &c.	
" 26.5.16	Inspected all animals of 72 Brigade & 73 Field Ambulance. Strong of 72nd Machine Gun Company require also Jackentine. Condition & general good. Hing of 72 M. Gun Coy & most Rank + not quile so good as others. Visited 72 Field Ambulance 15 cars across Pa another Subcivilleny Shoes & Att.D. horse.	

WAR DIARY
or
INTELLIGENCE SUMMARY.

Army Form C. 2118.

Hour, Date, Place	Summary of Events and Information	Remarks and references to Appendices
BAILLEUL. 26.5.16 (cont'd)	H.D. Hone. Temp. home. Investigation Ambulances Lymphatic broad who discharge from testicle. Arrived in good condition in morning. B&ff carried on pulling a head down & trestle of things strap netting the floors. Case isolated. Officer heartily empowered provided for Lymphatic breakwater of 1st Army. Visited 72 Field Ambulance & talked with Matron who recovered or	
27.5.16	26" inst. Pte S4/139787/Pte H.M. LEWINGTON A.S.C. arrived to take no 15663/Hospl. Rogers. E.M. M.C. Cheif to PARIS to take his transferred to Schrittle Veterinary Section private. No 746. Sergt Appleby C.E. AVC 36th V Section signed on for duration of war (A.F. W 3125) on 26" inst & proceeded on his month furlough to ENGLAND this day. Visited 3 F.M.V.Section at	
28.5.76	Visited 72 Field Ambulance. Veg-time M. acting in case Matrons absence. Arranged to attendance of sick changes of O.C. 10th N. Stafford marching Regt Bailleul and hospital to proceed. Visited 142 H. Battery R.G.A. Returned A.A.F Book as G.O.C. n-a army. ab	

WAR DIARY or INTELLIGENCE SUMMARY

Army Form C. 2118.

Hour, Date, Place	Summary of Events and Information	Remarks and references to Appendices
BAILLEUL 29-5-16	Inspected with O.C. Divisional Train the 73rd Sqdn. Brigade. Civilian forage goods & stores that May had been new torrid after pressed. There was tendency to turn the hulls of the sieves the hulls but here anyhow. D.S.V.C. & D.A.C. and the sample spent. 50% spelt contained seeds about 2nd key removed with trestles, heaters arrival unisex. found but at the post here the same. Same letters for a lime freshly. Inspecting dejected fruits, none has occurred. The seed is supposed to belong to the Fennel family of Ptain STEENWERCK Station and Fam. le entraining for and arrived from No 3 Sqn. V Section.	
" 30-5-16	Visited D.D.V.S. 2 Army Start with he a sample of the oats previously mentioned. There has been no critic or any ill-effects noticed from its use.	
" 31-5-16	Inspected with O.C. Divisional Train the animals D/15 "Shrapnel" Forester. Animals Condition fair but dull, & feel required attention.	

WAR DIARY
or
INTELLIGENCE SUMMARY.
(Erase heading not required.)

Army Form C. 2118.

Hour, Date, Place	Summary of Events and Information	Remarks and references to Appendices
	Martin	
Bailleul. 31.5.16 (Cont)	Visited 194 and 197 Companies A.S.C. & saw some horses just out from Reserve Parks at 1st Corps for work. Their condition generally was indifferent and some exhibiting symptoms as fit for work. Visited I Corps Heavy Artillery Group and investigated an outbreak of the among H.A. Horses. There were twelve (12) cases and three (3) cases fatal. While cause is attributed to over-damp picketines, where other they enter for a day, with the result that the horses all frequently rolled in. The cause received this influence in more but died the large Klistin were largely infected with the Bacterium Tetracaute horses.	
	Reference to DDVS. 2 Army. S.O.C.I. Corps. H.A. Group. 2nd Division. A.L.	

CONFIDENTIAL.

WAR DIARY
OF
A.D.V.S. 24ᵀᴴ DIVISION.

From 1-6-16 To 30-6-16.

Volume 10.

Army Form C. 2118.

WAR DIARY
or
INTELLIGENCE SUMMARY. ADVS - 24TH DIVISION

(Erase heading not required.)

Instructions regarding War Diaries and Intelligence Summaries are contained in F. S. Regs., Part II. and the Staff Manual respectively. Title pages will be prepared in manuscript.

Hour, Date, Place	Summary of Events and Information	Remarks and references to Appendices
Bailleul 1-6-16	Visited O.C. V Corps Heavy Artillery Group made arrangt with reference to the outbreak of Colic in his Group. Left at Mob: office 2 hid clinics for 3rd & 5th Siege Battys. R.H.A. Visited 196 Company I.S.C. with O.C. Div. Train inspected some horses sent up from Base Reserve Park. Visited O.C. 24 DAC with reference to consignment of oats containing oats of weed seeds much - recommended them like thoroughly cleaned & one sack of affected to be mixed with 3 not much of Sound clean oats. The digestive trouble has occurred up from feeding with that consignment. DDVS. 2nd Army asked. Told him about Colic (Flatulent) in V Corps H.A.Group. Arranged with Y.M.C.A. Views then manager for a Conference of ADS'S - 2nd Army on Saturday 3rd inst. Despatched war Diaries to A.G. Base and copies to O/c Records AMC Woolwich (Nos 4-9 dates 1st to 31/5/16). ah	
" 2-6-16	Visited 36 h.V.S. and 107 Bac (now Mob Section D.A.C)	

WAR DIARY
or
INTELLIGENCE SUMMARY.
(Erase heading not required.)

Army Form C. 2118.

Hour, Date, Place	Summary of Events and Information	Remarks and references to Appendices
BAILLEUL 2-6-16 (Cont'd)	No 2 Section DAC). Found that hubs and lugs are being turned. Also too much marking grease with Ewart and nails. Asked the DDVS in connection with this action. Weekly Conference of Veterinary officers. Foreman Skin disease is being - protected. The program will Mule put. Prepared A.F.A. 2002. ab	
" 3-6-16	Conference of A.D.V.S. 2nd Army, at BAILLEUL. Points discussed. Recent substitution of Oats. Chic crosses arising from rash, and amended lucerne, Emaciation. Quick Mauve Trades. Surplus ANC. Loan of Veterinary personnel for division. Hourly interview with G.O.C. Division aspects worth prospecting - actions taken. ab	
" 4-6-16	Visited 36th Veterinary Section, and recently armed Heavy Battery R.H.A. No 155. Their CO. all the important instruction relating to animals present. There were a certain amount of breast harness galls due to their new harness and soft animals. but G.O.C. I Corp H.A. Group is done lines. Cleos Minumel. ab Report Type.	

WAR DIARY
or
INTELLIGENCE SUMMARY

Army Form C. 2118.

(Erase heading not required.)

Instructions regarding War Diaries and Intelligence Summaries are contained in F.S. Regs., Part II. and the Staff Manual respectively. Title pages will be prepared in manuscript.

Hour, Date, Place	Summary of Events and Information	Remarks and references to Appendices
BAILLEUL 4-6-16 (Cont'd)	Type. Sent in one animal to M.V.S. for killing. This was unsuccessful from Remounts. Instructed to send in a Veterinary Note with any animals evacuated for the second time.	
5-6-16	Visited ADVS 50' Division in connection with evacuation of sick. DADVS attached 50' Division.	
6-6-16	In re ADVS to I Corps Commander re an Arts/mobile Vety Section of 50' Division. Went to STEENWERCK STATION to see sick animals entrained for Base. Visited 155 th Battery R.G.A. arranged with dating with Gunlim (when animal hospital huts) also horses of this unit.	
7-6-16	Visited 1st H Batt. R.G.A. 2 Section 151 Animals (2 horses). Visited B/106 Batty (106 Brigade R.F.A.). Found animals slightly improved. Examined 14 horses for Peristaltic Mange. 2 doubtful and one found. Reported to Divisional Headquarters + CRA that this Unit did not get the supervision they require. Some 70% Army production referring to treatment + disinfection plant for Sarcoptic & Mange. Copy of same sent to ADVS 2 Army + CRA.	

Forms/C. 2118/11

Army Form C. 2118.

WAR DIARY
or
INTELLIGENCE SUMMARY.
(Erase heading not required.)

Hour, Date, Place	Summary of Events and Information	Remarks and references to Appendices
BAILLEUL 7-6-16 (cont'd)	CRA Lt. Morrison was hurt & improperly equipt - knew not properties - & the men only 56 they have for 12 S. Horses. Arival here shews her still not properly geared. Visited b" Siege Battery R.G.A. oh	
" 8-6-16	Visited 36th V. Section Reported absence for RTCorps 2 L.D. Horses attached 17th Dividers - wages on point. Visited No 3 Section D.A.C.	
" 9-6-16	Smashed Stein Cases from B/110 B 3rd R.F.A. and 72nd Machine Gun Company, of DVS visited 36th h. V. Section - apparent to Entrophies with the Condition of the Section. Reported State of Division - & the cord of horses Kh inn. Conference of F.O.C. Veterinarian J/A.F.A. 2000. Remarks on state of horses Prevention of Evacuation oh	
" 10-6-16	Horses of 135 H.D. oth. R.G.A. by this month from Inglewing Jumander reports to D.D.V.S. 2 Army. Having interview with G.O.C. told him	

Form C. 2118/11.

WAR DIARY
or
INTELLIGENCE SUMMARY.
(Erase heading not required.)

Army Form C. 2118.

Hour, Date, Place	Summary of Events and Information	Remarks and references to Appendices
BAILLEUL 10.6.16 (Cont'd)	Took kits	
" 11-6-16.	the condition of B/108 Bde R.F.A. Superior not yet appointed, action taken regarding rather change of Visited 3 Rifle Battery R.G.A. Inspected recently arrived Remounts. A different class - poor in condition. 36th Mobile Vet Section turned out in marching order with Transport - Inspected by Col. Doyle AA + QMG and seen by DDVS 2nd Army. The whole turn out - Horses, Transport, Men, Equipment in good order.	
" 12-6-16	Visited 3 Fd M.V.S. and animals attached at WESTHOF Farm near NEUVE EGLISE.	
" 13-6-16	Inspected with V.O. Hr animals of V Corps H.A. Group. 30 animals - including two horses evacuated by 34 M.V.S. as	
" 14-6-16	Visited B108 Bde R.F.A. found animals improved in condition. Sent the new Veterinary Charge into 3 Fd M.V. Section. Disinfection measures are being carried out. Visited D/107 Bde R.F.A. Three cases with suspicious Skin Lesions had	

WAR DIARY
~~INTELLIGENCE SUMMARY~~
(Erase heading not required.)

Army Form C. 2118.

Hour, Date, Place	Summary of Events and Information	Remarks and references to Appendices
BAILLEUL. 14-6-16 (Cont'd)	has Evacuated - hospitals here found. Mr Arnould Mr. Baker are in good condition when visited on as sign of any skin disease.	
" 15-6-16	Visited the Section of No 2 D.A.C at MONT NOIR attached to 50 Division - Some teams here from skinny signs of over-work. Applied to O.C. 2nd D.A.C. who has arranged to change teams & give the drivers a rest. at/ Visited 92 and 73 Field Ambulances and No 4 Sect. D.A.C Saw AA Ophth regarding men of 73rd Infantry Brigade who "G.S.O." Divisional there and 1st Australian Infantry Brigade who are Original there. Arranged with ADMSs 50 Division and 2nd ANZAC Division for veterinary attendance to their brigades. at/	
" 16-6-16	Visited with O.C. No DAC No 2 Section. Transport Animals here in fair condition & some have thin. Examined the case for ADML1, & made recommendations as regards O Theins. Inspected Transport Animals of 73rd Infantry Brigade before leaving area. AS	

Army Form C. 2118.

WAR DIARY
or
INTELLIGENCE SUMMARY.
(Erase heading not required.)

Instructions regarding War Diaries and Intelligence
Summaries are contained in F. S. Regs., Part II.
and the Staff Manual respectively. Title pages
will be prepared in manuscript.

Hour, Date, Place	Summary of Events and Information	Remarks and references to Appendices
Bailleul 16.6.16 (cont'd)	Weekly conference of Veterinary Officers representatives of A.F.A. 2020. 03.	
17-6-16	There was a gas attack on the front on night of 16th inst. early morning of 17th inst. Reports which state that 16 H.D. and 6 L.D. horses and one Charger being away). These animals were seen to die with nothing further and transfer'd 14 H.D. belong to 19's Cy A.S.R. and 6 L.D. Changer & 17 Machine Gun Company. From case of H.D. here severely affected — respiration between 40 × 50. Serous discharge from nostrils. Temperature between 103 × 104. Pulse full, irregular and palpitating. Sounds perceptible. Conjunctival M.M. injected. M.M. Mouth & tongue slightly cyanotic. It would have been deemly stated these animals after taking Turpsel have bright red Trangas lines as quickly as possible as they were a recent open with them. The reaction was responsible for the laboured distressing symptoms. In case Cough regard dead r Lot) Schwy plain Subestands cone for truth.	

WAR DIARY
or
INTELLIGENCE SUMMARY.
(Erase heading not required.)

Army Form C. 2118.

Hour, Date, Place	Summary of Events and Information	Remarks and references to Appendices
BAILLEUL. 17-6-16 (Cont).	ward. Inclement. Rest. Stopped from + given trays as much relies as wish desired. Petulation of beg Othmer but have tried but gave practically no relief. The worst cases here have been the injuries. Vein this extend, gave to bed death. About 5 pricks of plexs have been necessary. Trench extend, seemed easier brights afternoon. Hypodermic injection of Strychnine have suggested, but is hopeful that this may heasen to inspiration which are already very laboured as 7hm hit bed. Now coma looks like dying during tonight. ob	
" 18-6-16	Visited the gener H.D. He seemed better + the most severe cases of the Sums discharge from hostile have ceased. At about... Into red here one all time green image. Sent in a preliminary report to DDVS. 2nd Army. Reported urgently Rep. O.C. Division. Arranged with OC for execution of one 13/106 see R.F.A. dr. in oleo front lines of standings + picking up + disinfection of Horses + standings. This is being effected with mange.	

WAR DIARY
or
INTELLIGENCE SUMMARY

Army Form C. 2118.

Hour, Date, Place	Summary of Events and Information	Remarks and references to Appendices
Bailleul 18-6-16 (contd)	heat. Visited ADVS 41st Division. He came out. Went back for an Mountie regarding his treatment of grand animals. Left mule with his clerk but Heeling letter first to pass with what forwarder. hospital ranks. Visited 36th V. Section. Saw Lt. Towle AVC with regard to games cases of 17" machine gun company. Suggested sentinels. Ches to regards to guns which ripped an animal from the Veterinary Officer. Saw O.C. 36th V.Section regarding new method of evacuating sick animals beyond. at	
19-6-16	Visited 19 s Cy ASC Tunnel 8 cases of goes poisoning his field. Visited 36th V.S. and ADVS. 41st Division. Took O.C. 36th V.S. and N.C.O. en route to execution of sick by Lt. W.A. MACGREGOR-A.VC Signed Secret Agreement from. 2nd Anzac Inf.y brigade arrived. 7 Anzac Inf. Bde on 16th Inst. et	

WAR DIARY
or
INTELLIGENCE SUMMARY.
(Erase heading not required.)

Army Form C. 2118.

Hour, Date, Place	Summary of Events and Information	Remarks and references to Appendices
20-6-16. BAILLEUL	16" wid.	
21-6-16 "	Visited 7" Aug. Stanh. Brigade & gazed cases at B'G.rd. These are improving at B.rea cases is purely ht hi their sign of weing lung trouble.	
22-6-16 "	Visited 1/1 Nunro R.H.A and 142 H.Bah R.G.A. at Le Tou. 167 Home & 150 H.Bh-R.G.A. Visited 17 Infantry Brigade Wagon lines at Say 62 Remonts arriv. Some officers L.D. Horses were with	
23-6-16 "	poor in Condition & Shewing signs of the mules indifferent. Heary Conference of M.O's in preparation of A.A.F.A 2000. 159 H.Batly. R.G.A. arrived at	
24. 6.16 "	Attended Carding parade with DDVS- 2nd Army. Visited No 3 Sect. S.A.C 3rd Siege Batty. 11" Labour Batty at	
25- 6-16 "	Visited 17 Infantry Brigade and Machine Gun Company. The Helmets has had on one Officers Charge of 1st R.F. whilst with Sergt Rinaldi. Horse was milked back i helmet, other Horses of the same was perfectly kind.	

WAR DIARY
or
INTELLIGENCE SUMMARY.
(Erase heading not required.)

Army Form C. 2118.

Hour, Date, Place	Summary of Events and Information	Remarks and references to Appendices
BAILLEUL. 25-6-16 (cond)	Arranged with A.D.V.S. 50 Division for Temporary attendance to 17th Infantry Brigade.	
" 26-6-16	Visited 159 H.Battery R.G.A under 166 Howrs. Began an endeavour temporarily to find position & forward to other lines at	
" 27-6-16	Visited H.Q. O.C.I. Coyn. H.A. Group with reference to begin lines of 159 Benty R.G.A. at	
" 28-6-16	Visited 106 Bde R.F.A. B. Batty had improved. Stationary horse been dentilated dug up & dried when wet in time took themsf & animals out in open. Other had improved. Sent in areas when the skin did not look well, no possible trial, but temporarily be evacuated but the C.O. of Brigade to next round their homes with me. ch	
" 29-6-16	Conference of A.D.S. 2nd Army at BAILLEUL. Discussed prevention by normal & special form, & gauge. Remarks on Helmeth to accent gas attack.	

WAR DIARY
INTELLIGENCE SUMMARY.
(Erase heading not required.)

Army Form C. 2118.

Hour, Date, Place	Summary of Events and Information	Remarks and references to Appendices
Brillwl. 29.6.16	Gas attack. It difficult to arrange having helmets with hose, men are not allowed forn. gas tomorrow during the attack. Some have shed P. helmet & then don't. The helmet is drawn on eyes, the others has not and when not stuck to airwards inside causing sloth greatly difficulty in breathing. The helmet must before inside by some time the inside water. Visited 36 b/N.F.S explained to C.O. When again I preventire expecient him under arrangements made for each person by to B.D.M.S 2nd Army. This is in addition to the evacuation by Road at 	
" 30.6.16	Visited 9/107 Bn R.F.A. inspected knew apparency a case of Skin disease (not parasitic) admitted to 36 b/H.S found at home Men healthy, in Good condition. Visited 3 th Berlin selected Cases. Prevention by Room i Raid melation. Visited annual Oplum R. v Bn. Signals at WEST not Farm.	

Army Form C. 2118.

WAR DIARY
or
INTELLIGENCE SUMMARY

(Erase heading not required.)

Instructions regarding War Diaries and Intelligence Summaries are contained in F. S. Regs., Part II. and the Staff Manual respectively. Title pages will be prepared in manuscript.

Hour, Date, Place	Summary of Events and Information	Remarks and references to Appendices
Bailleul. 30-6-16 (Cont.)	9 am. Weekly enterance Returns officers Proceeded in 9/A.F. A2010. Moved at 7.0's. of new arrangements for the evacuation Sick. D.D.M.S. 2nd Army called. Visits A.D.S. 50 Division reference A/ports Brigade attached.	

CONFIDENTIAL

WAR DIARY

OF

A.D.V.S. 24ᵀᴴ DIVISION.

From 1-7-16 To 31-7-16.

Volume. II.

WAR DIARY of A.D.V.S. 24th DIVISION

INTELLIGENCE SUMMARY

Army Form C. 2118.

(Erase heading not required.)

Hour, Date, Place	Summary of Events and Information	Remarks and references to Appendices
Bailleul. 1-7-16	Forwarded War Diary for June 1916 to A.G.'s Office, Base, and A.F.B.158. to O/C Records - A.V.C. Base. The DDVS has recommended to the Q.M.G. that no further provision of smoke helmets for horses shall be made. (DDVS-2nd Army No V 107 d 29.6.16) Medical Officers met G.O.C. Division. Lt. Stewart. P.S. M.V.C. left 41st H.B. R.G.A. on transfer to Office i/c DDVS. 2nd Army, the honour now to held J.L. Sullivan. M.V.S. at 142 H.Bty. R.G.A. 73 Field Ambulance. New Area at Loere. 36 Mobile Veterinary Section.	
3.7.16	From midnight this Division was transferred to IX Corps. New Billet for 36 M.V.S. at S.8.B.2.9 Near Bailleul.	Sheet 28.
4.7.16 p.m.	Division moved to LOCRE. Sergt. TURNELL. A.V.C. (No 1633) arrived LOCRE, sent in to join 17 Infantry Brigade. See Sergt Guy Kangust a recommendation for a commission. Visited @ 109 inspected newly arrived of Battery as in case of	

LOCRE

WAR DIARY
or
INTELLIGENCE SUMMARY.

(Erase heading not required.)

Army Form C. 2118.

Hour, Date, Place	Summary of Events and Information	Remarks and references to Appendices
LOCRE 4.7.16 (Cnt'd)	Class IT horses manoeuvred for lameness. All horses were clean & groomed & have new ditches. Put before cases for observation & dressing. Visited all sections of the S.M.R.	
" 5.7.16	Visited B/109. B106. No.1 & 2 Companies A.C.C. M.M.P. and A106. at	
" 6.7.16	Visited D107. B108 and C108.	
" 7.7.16	Visited 106 Bde R.F.A. hurriedly. Conference of Veterinary Officers at our preparation of A.F. H.Z000. A.D.V.S. posted to R.F.A Brigades under new organization of All Artillery units having Field areas &	
" 8.7.16	heavily in service with 9 O.C. Received instructions to report Veterinary attendance to IX Corps Cavalry Reft. Visited A.B Squadrons 1/1st R.Wilts Yeomanry and C Squadron 1/1st Herts Carbineers and H.Qm & Regiment - horses to be seen to & the Mob Squadrons. horses & two Mules of 1/1st Herts are to form cadres. Reported matters to DDVS. 2nd Army & also remarked that every Trench & Mule attached to the division to IX Corps Cavalry Reft were not yet the	
" 9.7.16		

WAR DIARY
or
INTELLIGENCE SUMMARY.

Army Form C. 2118.

Hour, Date, Place	Summary of Events and Information	Remarks and references to Appendices
LOCRE. 9-7-16 (Cont'd)	attention from a divisional veterinary Officer but they require under their present Staff. 30 lot of medicines left Div. outpatient Kennel.	
" 10.7.16 Bailleul	36 M.V.S. evacuated before move to Bailleul. Divisional Headquarters moved to BAILLEUL. Arranged with Division and 41st Division for 36 M.V.S. to move to Flea Cabrel at B.1 d.g.3 (Sheet 36) the billet being in shelter. Division billeting area.	
" 11-7-16	36 M.V. Section moved to B.1 d.g.3 (Sheet 36). D.D.V.S. 2nd Army paid us a visit. Capt. H.K. Barron A.V.C. II Corps Cavalry Regt. took over the IX Corps Cavalry Regt. billets. O.C. IX Corps Cavalry Regt. was Capt. Barron.	
" 12-7-16	Visited 159 H.Batty. R.G.A. Found a number of cases of cow-pox. 150 H.Batty. R.G.A. Found 3 cow-pox men which were isolated. Found a charger belonging to Capt. J.R. Stansfeld R.G.A. 147 H.Batty R.G.A. with Border Horse in a field occupied by 41st Div. Supply Column.	

WAR DIARY
or
INTELLIGENCE SUMMARY.
(Erase heading not required.)

Army Form C. 2118.

Hour, Date, Place	Summary of Events and Information	Remarks and references to Appendices
BAILLEUL 12.7.16 (Cont'd)	Adieu-	
13.7.16	Lieu FLÊTRE. Horse sent to 3 Sqn. V Section and Officer notified at Visited 3 Sqn. V Section. 194 Cpl Neele inspected Surplus H.D. Horses. Horse sent to 3 Sqn V Section to await disposal. Visited 73 Infantry Brigade. MO 1DD V S - 2nd Army in BAILLEUL arranged hereunder enter for animals affected at	
14.7.16	hastily conference Veterinary Officers. Remarks on Mange in Equidae. General detection. Farriers to Equidae Offices in all opinion of Surgeon Lieut. Lt J.L. Sullivan AVC 41st 4A Bde Tn.R an Officer Walker. Detailed Captain J. Blackburn AVC to veterinary charge of 20th M.Rs r Derby Return Bells at	
15.7.16	Visited IX Corps Cavalry Regiment - evacuated 6 horses suspicious Mange for B Squadron. Capt Brown AVC 70½ commenced Malleining of his regiment. 36th V S evacuation B.case by Barge from ESTAIRES. Inspected B/16b. evacuated 12 cases Mange - referred 11 slight cases	

WAR DIARY
or
INTELLIGENCE SUMMARY.

Army Form C. 2118.

Hour, Date, Place	Summary of Events and Information	Remarks and references to Appendices
Bailleul 15.7.16 (Cont'd)	Ship/Canals.	
	Interview with C. Stephens Station.	
	Visited DDVS. 2nd Army to get two drivers of C. Stephens Station.	
	Headquarters. with G.O.C. remarks that March. restored the	
	necessity of have men to look after B106 as animals are not	
	Employment. G.O.C. still thyme here are men to two stretch	
	advanced & men in R.Y & list at	
16.7.16	Visited 36th V. Section - Evacuated 59 cases by Road.	
	Visited No 2 Sect. no DAC sent in two cases Vetlin for examination.	
	Proceeded to METEREN MORRIS & OUTERSTEENE & inspected 2 H.D.	
	with 3rd Infantry Brigade . 1st Australian Division. No one anxious	
PM.	to find although all the farms in the neighbourhood have visited.	
	Visited 30th A.V.S. which had 11 stream cases, was the incredible	
	troops on 17th had also arranged for Stretcher Sqn H.D. q 3rd Infantry	
	Bde. 1st Australian Division. at	
17.7.16	3L.H.F.S. evacuated 11 cases by range from ESTAIRES.	
"	Proceeded THIENSOUK & saw S.home of action at farm.	

WAR DIARY
or
INTELLIGENCE SUMMARY

Army Form C. 2118.

Hour, Date, Place	Summary of Events and Information	Remarks and references to Appendices
BAILLEUL. 17.7.16 (Cont'd)	from. At her bil Read. Hughes stayed for the hour duration of 139 Field Ambulance. 41st Division which has front down. Saw O.C. Field Ambulance from the hour (Major Fabrig's unit) Managed McKelvie. Have Rovers from No2 furnished tomorrow. Then Mr. office to Branch Requisition Office - 2nd Army. Visited C104 - Brig. B108- B107 Bn Return. BTMS. 2nd Army cabled and arranged for selling of excess fat for fed to treat A Battern. Reported Cross Group Sanitary Officer BAILLEUL 16 Army Commandant II Corps for D.D.M.S. to execute state precautions by Visited 3 C.M.S. and 18 Trackment 2nd Cavalry Division.	
" 18.7.16	Returned returned protein of 52 H.A Brigade 17D. & 1st Anzac H.A. G. Head Sunters.	
" 19.7.16	Interviewed G.O.C. Division about an outgrown of herps examined soldiers at Canadian Battalion - Bailleul - no evidence of private infection.	

WAR DIARY or INTELLIGENCE SUMMARY

Army Form C. 2118.

Hour, Date, Place	Summary of Events and Information	Remarks and references to Appendices
BAILLEUL. 19-7-16 (cont'd)	Inspection.	
	6.10 am encountered refugees from BAC ST MAUR by 36 A.V.S. Other cars for men. Visited A.D.T.S.- 41st Division filled one sick from 36 A.V.S. they knew time to evacuate before moving. ad	
ST JANS CAPPEL. 20.7.16	Moved to ST JANS CAPPEL. A.D.V.S. 20th Division called & informed him of unit attached to Division in area. Interview G.O.C. Division on matters relating to transport and stores. ad	
21.7.16	Visited 17th 72nd & 73rd Infantry Brigades Areas. ad	
22.7.16	Visited Flanning units D/106, C/107, No1 Company A.S.C. B/107. B/105, A/106 and C/108 hastily interview with G.O.C. Division & drew up chapter on whelping Inspection of Mange - Same particulars in Divisional Orders. ad	
23.7.16	Inspected 54 Remounts at CAESTRE. 6x rejected for Regrounds. Visited 195 & 197 Companies A.S.C. and B/108. Gave order from G.O.C.3rd Bn & Section & shell. same surrendered by O.C. 36 A.V.S. ad	
24.7.16	Division commenced entraining for area S/of the SOMME.	

Army Form C. 2118.

WAR DIARY
or
INTELLIGENCE SUMMARY.
(Erase heading not required.)

Instructions regarding War Diaries and Intelligence Summaries are contained in F.S. Regs., Part II. and the Staff Manual respectively. Title pages will be prepared in manuscript.

Hour, Date, Place	Summary of Events and Information	Remarks and references to Appendices
SOMME.		
St Jans Cappel. 24.7.16 (cont'd)	Proceed to Amiens en route to new area. Arrived Amiens 6 p.m. Whilst discharging station at Saleux and Longeaux saw transport of 19th Infantry Brigade disentrain also.	
Amiens 25.7.16	Left Amiens.	
Amiens Cavillon	Arrived Cavillon. Reported arrival and location of 36 H.V. Section to DDVS - 4th Army, & asked for instructions regarding disposal of sick.	
" 26-7-16	Remainder of D.H.Q. and 36 H.V. Section arrived Cavillon. Head quarters Infantry Brigade Areas and Artillery Areas with it. DAA & QMG cy	
" 27.7.16	Visited Heavy Artillery Brigade & interviewed V.O.'s & at each:— 106. 107. 108. 109 and D.A.C cy	
" 28.7.16	Visited 72 Infantry Brigade Area. Received wire from A/DVS/4 Army (civil) with Maure at Riencourt. Visited same named unit. Whole in village - no British Army animals near billets. Weekly Conference of V.O's & preparation of weekly states. cy	

Army Form C. 2118.

WAR DIARY
or
INTELLIGENCE SUMMARY.
(Erase heading not required.)

Instructions regarding War Diaries and Intelligence Summaries are contained in F. S. Regs., Part II. and the Staff Manual respectively. Title pages will be prepared in manuscript.

Hour, Date, Place	Summary of Events and Information	Remarks and references to Appendices
CAILLORS. 28.7.16 (Cont'd)	State.	
29.7.16	Whilst 72 M.G. Company 109 Bde R.F.A Captain T.F. Donworth A.V.C. attached 109 Bde R.F.A accidentally drowned in evening of 28th inst. helped DDVS. Fourth Army amphibia for a whip. Senr. Adjutant 109 Bde re disposal of personal Kit - case of Armament Veterinary Equipment for Mrs D.O. Visit to 109 Bde R.F.A. most with O.C. (Capt. Goodwin) to ascertain accident happened (Drony). Sweep with O.C. Division. Casualties eprs of DVS Ci News No.17 d 27.3.15 ~ DDVS Fourth Army No.1167 d 28.7.16 Total Veterinary officers at	
30.7.16	Visit 1st, 12 Royal Fusiliers. 3rd Rifle Brigade. 106 Bde R.F.A 23rd Infantry Brigade and 15 "Sherwood Forresters. Orders for "G" Passed To Pargnes Town or 3rd unit. DAORS area.	
31.7.16	Moved To CORBIE. Reported arrival to DDVS. 4 Army.	

Army Form C. 2118.

WAR DIARY
or
INTELLIGENCE SUMMARY

(Erase heading not required.)

Hour, Date, Place	Summary of Events and Information	Remarks and references to Appendices
CORBIE. 31.7.16 (cont'd)	4th Army. 36th V.S. arrived CORBIE.	

CONFIDENTIAL.

24/ ADVS 242 Vol 12

WAR DIARY

OF

A.D.V.S. 24TH DIVISION

FROM 1-8-16 TO 31-8-16.

VOLUME (12).

Army Form C. 2118.

WAR DIARY
or
INTELLIGENCE SUMMARY.
(Erase heading not required.)

ADVS. 24th Division

Instructions regarding War Diaries and Intelligence Summaries are contained in F. S. Regs., Part II. and the Staff Manual respectively. Title pages will be prepared in manuscript.

Hour, Date, Place	Summary of Events and Information	Remarks and references to Appendices
CORBIE 1-8-16	Lieut J.R. Barker, A.V.C. (T.C.) reported his arrival to O.C. 109 Brigade R.F.A. on the evening of 31.7.16, and further orders today, gave him instruction as regards duties.	
" 2-8-16	Visited Divisional Artillery at DAOURS and VECQUEMONT. at Capt CORBIE. 36th V Section left 1 N.C.O. & 3 men until R.A. here.	
FORKED TREE 2-8-16	Arrived FORKED TREE and 36th V.S. arrived later in day. Notified DDVS. 5th Army & Signals terminal.	L 2 Bq 2 Sh17 62D NE.
" 3-8-16	Left Advanced Collecting Station at FORKED TREE - 36th V.S. moved to BOIS de TAILLES K12. R.A. arrived Bois de Tailles at K12 Sh17 62D NE	
" 4-8-16	Visited R.A. huts at	
" 5-8-16	held enquiry of Veterinary Officer Morphurlin of A.F.A. 2009 at Visited 107 Bde R.F.A. and Advanced Creating Station of	
" 6-8-16	Visited DDVS. 2nd Army at QUERRIEU, and No 12 M.V.S. at Railhead at MÉRICOURT L'ABBÉ.	
" 7-8-16	Visited F. Ambulance huts at DIVES COPSE.	of J24 b. Sh17 62D NE

WAR DIARY
or
INTELLIGENCE SUMMARY.
(Erase heading not required.)

Army Form C. 2118.

Instructions regarding War Diaries and Intelligence Summaries are contained in F. S. Regs., Part II. and the Staff Manual respectively. Title pages will be prepared in manuscript.

Hour, Date, Place	Summary of Events and Information	Remarks and references to Appendices
FORKED TREE - 8-8-16	Visited Divisional Train.	
" 9-8-16	Sergt T. LITHERLAND A.V.C. arrived and attached to B/106 Brigade R.F.A. vice Sergt LINTORN A.V.C. evacuated sick.	
	Visited No 12 M.V.S. refuses increase for sick animals. Received at MERICOURT L'ABBE impelled S.S. Remounts.	F.21.b. Sh.w.62 D NE
" 10-8-16	Visited CITADEL. Saw A.D.V.S. 2nd Division regarding position of M.V.S. Issued instructions regarding evacuation of sick lame & tired. Lightning actions are in the neighbourhood of Chien Brown. 2nd Divisional M.V.S. at L.9.central.	} Sh.w.62 D NE
	" - Advanced - L.3.A.6.4	
	" - Main - R.12	
	" - M.V.S. - MEAULTÉ E.17.c.7.9	
" 11-8-16	Visited MEAULTÉ, saw position of 53rd M.V.S. which will be taken over by No 36 M.V. Section. Near conference of 110" preparation of A.F.A2002.	
" 12-8-16	Visited CITADEL saw A.D.V.S. 5th Division.	
CITADEL 13-8-16	Moved 16 CITADEL and 36 M.V. Section to MEAULTÉ	F.21.b. Sh.w.62 D NE

WAR DIARY
or
INTELLIGENCE SUMMARY.

(Erase heading not required.)

Army Form C. 2118.

Hour, Date, Place	Summary of Events and Information	Remarks and references to Appendices
13.8.16 CITADEL		
14.8.16 "	R.A visit area to MEAULTÉ area at Visited 17th Infantry Brigade and 19th M. Gun Company & re-clear-fast turn-out pack 16 L.D. at	
15.8.16 "	Visited 93rd Infantry Brigade - 24" D.A.C A+B/109 die R.F.A + 36th V. Section at	
16.8.16 "	Attended Conference of A.D's V.S. Fourth Army at Toutencourt L'Abbé. Discussed evacuation of sick. Gas effects & protection of againsts animals. Watering arrangements of mounted Army Corps.	
17.8.16 "	Visited 73rd Inf. Brigade & Daujt: Horse hospital in R. and 36th V. Section at	
18.8.16 "	Visited CORBIE and inspected 73 and 74 Field Ambulances and a veterinary case from 74 Field Ambulance to 36th V.S. Held Conference of Veterinary Officers and preparation of A.F. A2000 at	
19.8.16 .	Visited 17, 72, -73 Infantry Brigades Bella V.S. Despatches handed mine to DDVS Fourth Army at	

WAR DIARY
INTELLIGENCE SUMMARY

Army Form C. 2118.

Hour, Date, Place	Summary of Events and Information	Remarks and references to Appendices
CITADEL. 20-8-16	Visited B/108 Bde R.F.A. - D/108/- Bde R.F.A. Animals in B/108 are practically free from skin disease. Due chiefly for great attention of V.O. Mr Lieut. H. B. TOWELL A.V.C. DDVS found Army cobs at 36th. V. Section inspected declining animals & cases for evacuation. Inspected 56 Remounts at HERICOURT - L'ABBÉ. Mostly mules, all of a good class & in good condition. Camp of No.9 Bde R.F.A. bombed from aeroplanes - 17 horses injured. Saw with 1/36th. V. S. No animals killed & most of wounds open of the size that had never escaped notice. Kindness of	
" 21-8-16	"	
" 22.8.16	Met A DVS 20' Division & arranged relief of American M.S. Met DDVS. Fourth Army. Visited R.F.A. Infantry Transport Wagon lines at FORKED TREE.	
" 23.8.16	H.Qrs. Division moved to FORKED TREE. Visited 109 Bde R.F.A. and 36th. V. S.	

WAR DIARY
or
INTELLIGENCE SUMMARY

Army Form C. 2118.

Hour, Date, Place	Summary of Events and Information	Remarks and references to Appendices
FORKED TREE 24.8.16	Advanced checking party returned to 36th V.S. at Méaulte.	
BUIRE 25.8.16	H.Q. Division moved to Buire. Weekly Conference D.V.O's. Preparation I.A.F. A 2000. at Méaulte.	
" 26.8.16	Visited horse troughs at Méaulte. Some inadequate arrangements for regulating supply of water - ploughing horses & mules of animals watering (5000 mules daily). Some troughs were half full & a number of sahens and jutts, that have cleaned out since erection. No officer is in charge. Matter is most unsatisfactory, severely affecting the condition of animals. Reported to D.D.V.S. at K.Q.	
" 27.8.16	Visited D.D.V.S. Forest Army & submitted a minute report on watering of animals at Méaulte & discussed matter with him. Sent copy to Division for information. at	
" 28.8.16	Visited 36th V. Section and 72 - 73 - 94 Field Ambulances. at	

WAR DIARY
INTELLIGENCE SUMMARY.

Army Form C. 2118.

Hour, Date, Place	Summary of Events and Information	Remarks and references to Appendices
BUIRE 29-8-16	Visited 36th V. Section. Was present at making arrangements at MÉAULTE, & D.O. 1/c 108 Bde R.F.A. when horses are ridden. Have not yet heard as Traction Taken by South Army a regards his report of the 27th inst at Visited ADVS. 33rd Division & arranged position of Mobile Veterinary Section and to evacuate sick from that Division. Also arrange with ADVS. 14th Division to evacuate sick from that Division.	No. 6822. Sgr BETHEL HQrs from 134 Heavy Battery. R.G.A. III Corps H.A. Group joined D/108 Brigade R.F.A. vice Sgr Parker HQrs evacuated accidentally wounded.
" 30-8-16	Visited 36th V. Section.	
E MEAULTE 31-8-16	DHQ moved to headquarters vacated by 33rd Division at E... DDVS South Army notified. Made further report on watering arrangements at MÉAULTE — no improvement. Mules, horses, transport too Condition in animals.	62 NE.

(9.26.6) W 2794 160,000 8/14 H W V Forms/C. 2118/11

CONFIDENTIAL.

24/vol 13

WAR DIARY

OF

A.D.V.S. 24TH DIVISION

FROM 1-9-16 TO 30-9-16.

VOLUME 13

WAR DIARY or INTELLIGENCE SUMMARY.   ADVS. 24th DIVISION.

Army Form C. 2118.

Hour, Date, Place	Summary of Events and Information	Remarks and references to Appendices
E11 Central. 1-9-16	Visited 24 DAC and R.F.A. wagon lines. — 1st Cavalry Divn Auxiliary H.T. Company A.S.C. and 36th V. Section. Weekly Conference of V.Os and Preparation of A.F. A 2000. DDVS. Fourth Army called — head told him Four watering arrangements at Méaulte. There are troughs here have been erected and two new at present in use each Trough Shed holds abt 50 animals. Standing round troughs are fair also — approaches where present is a Sea of Mud — composed of chalk slime. Old troughs abt present in a bad state — approaches when frozen — troughs very dirty & a number are unserviceable.	Sheet 62D NE.
" 2-9-16	Visited 108 Bde R.F.A. inspected Veterinary Wallets, and No 4 Section 24 DAC at	
" 3-9-16	Visited 36th V. Section, and B/106 Bde R.F.A. – 2 Bn of Three animals were killed by shell dropped in wagon lines of 14 D.A.C. at present attached to 9th Division. 6 mules were killed and 15 wounded. Also visited 178 Tunnelling Company.	

WAR DIARY
or
INTELLIGENCE SUMMARY.
(Erase heading not required.)

Army Form C. 2118.

Instructions regarding War Diaries and Intelligence Summaries are contained in F. S. Regs., Part II. and the Staff Manual respectively. Title pages will be prepared in manuscript.

Hour, Date, Place	Summary of Events and Information	Remarks and references to Appendices
E 11 Central 4-9-16	helped ADVS. 55" Division finish attached for Veterinary attendance. This Division under Orders longer by road (mounted parties) diamond got by train. Detailed Lieut. J.R. BAKER. AVC to accompany Infantry transport to march. Capt. N.A. MACGREGOR. A.V.C. to accompany Divisional Train & other units.	
5-9-16	Orders issued to 36. M.V.S. to accompany second party proceeding by road to Ginist. at	
6-9-16	Visited R.A. lines at _____ R.E. lines _____ move to Bois des TAILLES. XIV Corps informed 24th Division Arty Artillery are attached to I Division. helped ADVS I Division. to arrange for Evacuation of sick. Sent copies of AFA 2000 for inclusion in V Division returns. helped Veterinary Officers to report to ADVS I Division at _____	
Ailly le Haut Clocher 7-9-16	Move to AILLY LE HAUT CLOCHER M.I.V.S. also traveled to same place. at	Map ABBEVILLE

Army Form C. 2118.

WAR DIARY
or
INTELLIGENCE SUMMARY.
(Erase heading not required.)

Instructions regarding War Diaries and Intelligence Summaries are contained in F. S. Regs., Part II. and the Staff Manual respectively. Title pages will be prepared in manuscript.

Hour, Date, Place	Summary of Events and Information	Remarks and references to Appendices
Ailly Le Haut Clocher 8-9-16	Veterinary Officer called at office - Superintendent of A.F.A 2000. ab	
9-9-16	Visited Infantry Brigades in Area ab	
10-9-16	Visited Field Ambulances ab	
11-9-16	Visited Machine Gun Companies. Inoculated Series of Debility from 17th M. Gun. Company. ab	
12-9-16	Divisional Horse & Transport Show - Animals were turned out. Condition good & clean. Horses well fitted no evidence Mange galls. There were ten concourse care & attention to animal & Transport. ab	
13-9-16	Visited 72nd and 17th Infantry Brigade ab	
14-9-16	Visited Three Companies of Divisional Train. ab	
15-9-16	Veterinary Officer called office - Superintendent of A.F.A 2000. ab	
16-9-16	Visited 73rd Infantry Brigade ab	

WAR DIARY or INTELLIGENCE SUMMARY

Army Form C. 2118.

Hour, Date, Place	Summary of Events and Information	Remarks and references to Appendices
Ailly Le HAUT CLOCHER. 17-9-16	17th Infantry Brigade Horse Transport Slow - Practically whole t Brigade Transport, Machine Gun Company, Pack Animals were Inspected. Turnout cleanliness & condition of animals good. Have report to DDVS Fourth Army re action taken with regard to Prevention of Horse disease" :- 1) Martin Order in D.O. 6 G.R.O 1135. 2) DRO 642, dated 25-4-16 Publishes warning re.b dropping from Conifers while on the march. Raid to extend from trees before being used as fuel. 3) IV Corps R.O. 467 dated 13.11.15 appendix n D.R.O 4) DRO No 1323 dated 13-9-16 Publishes "The markings from "pickets upraise" is one of the most serious causes of influence in animals. Attention is called to G.R.O 1135. D.R.O 642 dated 25-4-16. Boxes are to be fixed up at different places in villages refilling points and Ammunition Dumps, into which Horse Nails from Boxes &	

WAR DIARY
or
INTELLIGENCE SUMMARY

Army Form C. 2118.

Hour, Date, Place	Summary of Events and Information	Remarks and references to Appendices
Ailly le Haut Clocher 17-9-16 (Cont'd)	from boxes & gathered up from time to time in Wilton. These boxes are kept "Nails" in large letters to attract attention but only fits for one receptacle, but to attempt to reseach for actin the "Fitter hell" upon to baits Spam it's ground, et.	
18-9-16	Orders received for the Division to have Abt Army on 19" inst. Antipation Ard for 36th V. Section.	
BRUAY 19-9-16	Arrived BRUAY. at	Sheet 36 B 1/40,000
20-9-16	36 M.V. Section arrived PERNES at	"
	D.D.V.S. First Army and D.D.R. Cohen at	
21-9-16	Wiles 36th V. Section and 73 Infantry Brigade.	
22-9-16	Veterinary Officers asked. Preparation D/A.F.A. 20000 Field Slaughter Tractive and D.D.V.S. First Army. A.D.V.S. IX Division asked regarding the IX Division having its Divisional Artillery at	
23-9-16	36 A.V.S. hour to BRUAY. at	

Army Form C. 2118

WAR DIARY
or
INTELLIGENCE SUMMARY
(Erase heading not required.)

Instructions regarding War Diaries and Intelligence Summaries are contained in F.S. Regs., Part II. and the Staff Manual respectively. Title Pages will be prepared in manuscript.

Place	Date	Hour	Summary of Events and Information	Remarks and references to Appendices
BRUAY.	24-9-16		Visited CAMBLAIN L'ABBÉ r saw A.D.V.S. IX Division reference IX Division Arthkury. Veterinary Officer left behind, and attached Units, viz 1 36m. V.S. 1021 M.V.S. blek. at	Sheet 36B 1/40,000
"	25-9-16		Visited 36th V Section uno order to more to FRESNICOURT on 26th viz. The man Pole sent on Today 17h30 or behalf. at	"
CAMBLAIN L'ABBÉ	26-9-16		Move to CAMBLAIN L'ABBÉ. DDMS. IV Corps visited me with regard to arise of Rabies at Gouy SERVINS. Visited Gouy SERVINS with Tom MATOR and Marie investigated & forwarded report to DDVS. First Army. at	"
"	27-9-16		Visited 72 Field Ambulance and 36 M.V. Section and 104 Company A.S.C. IX Division regarding across Manage & to see what precautions are being Taken Fprevent contagion. at	"
"	28-9-16		Visited GAUCHIN-LEGAL and inspected 50 and 51 Brigades R.F.A. (IX Division). Capt. D. CAMPBELL. A.V.C. accompanied me. Found an animal with pair condition Evacuated Mc Cass A/51 Bde R.F.A. & Veterinary reasons. There was a deficiency of Shoghul i.e. 1 may Batting and had 1 Muhulet here Trimmed. at	"

Army Form C. 2118

WAR DIARY
or
INTELLIGENCE SUMMARY
(Erase heading not required.)

Instructions regarding War Diaries and Intelligence Summaries are contained in F.S. Regs., Part II. and the Staff Manual respectively. Title Pages will be prepared in manuscript.

Place	Date	Hour	Summary of Events and Information	Remarks and references to Appendices
CAMBLAIN L'ABBÉ	29-9-16		Held Conference of Veterinary Officers re preparation of A.F.A 2000. N Sergeant A.V.C having gone on leave without any reference to this appointee, has permitted 16 D.M.Q. third concerned. at	
"	30-9-16		Inspected 52nd Brigade R.F.A (9th Division) with V.O. Horses those of this Brigade is in fair Condition, but the practice of trimming held no general. Visited Divisional Train. at	

CONFIDENTIAL

WAR DIARY

OF

A.D.V.S. 24ᵀᴴ DIVISION

FROM 1-10-16 TO 31-10-16.

VOLUME 14

Army Form C. 2118

WAR DIARY
or
INTELLIGENCE SUMMARY

(Erase heading not required.)

ADMS 24th DIVISION

Place	Date	Hour	Summary of Events and Information	Remarks and references to Appendices
CAMBLAIN L'ABBÉ	1/10/16		Visited 24th Divisional Train, and three of M.M.P. and 50 Bde R.F.A. 9th Division at	
"	2/10/16		Visited 51st Bde R.F.A. at Gauchin Legal. Two horses sent to M.V.S. at	
"	3/10/16		Visited 52nd Bde R.F.A. at	
"	4/10/16		Visited 9th D.A.C. and 1 Company 9th Divisional Train, also bathing at Mont St Eloy and attachment Fowlis near Ecoivres. at	
"	5/10/16		9th Divisional Artillery returned to Division from operations on the Somme. Saw all units in rest and went round various battery lines at temporary standings. The animals had taken away in condition & very great numbers were very poor - About 250 animals will need to be evacuated. Few condition movement & want of rest - hard & campaign conditions.	

WAR DIARY
or
INTELLIGENCE SUMMARY

Army Form C. 2118

Place	Date	Hour	Summary of Events and Information	Remarks and references to Appendices
CAMBLAIN L'ABBÉ	6/10/16		Veterinary Officers with Artillery reported at this Office & received report. Arrived & behind in the French. Held Conference of Veterinary Officers preparatory to A.F.A. 2000. Artillery completed their re-organization making, by an Interview & absorbing 1st while A/101, B/101 Bde R.F.A. and A Bty 108 Bde R.F.A. Few surplus Sergeants A.V.C. sent to 36 D.V.S. to await orders. at	
"	7/10/16		Visited the Divisional Artillery units & gave instruction as regards evacuation of debilitated animals. Visits C/116 Bde R.F.A. at MONT S'ELOY & recommended 26 horses for evacuation. at	
"	8/10/16		Attended Conference of A.D's V.S. at Office of D.D.V.S. First Army. The following points were discussed:— Referring of F.O.M.S. with Artillery Units & Sept 6. A.V.C. Contribution to the Kitchener Memorial.	

WAR DIARY
or
INTELLIGENCE SUMMARY
(Erase heading not required.)

Army Form C. 2118

Place	Date	Hour	Summary of Events and Information	Remarks and references to Appendices
CAMBLAIN L'ABBÉ	8/10/16 (cont.)		Kitchener Memorial. The whole Veterinary Section 17th attached to Brigade - amounts to 1 Farr. S/S., 1 Shoeing Smith, 1 Cpl, 1 Pnr., three mules. (Note the mare on A.F.B. 2009 of arrival [illegible] missing). Drugs - no practically D.A.D.V.S. representing drugs to be renewed &c. A new cheap folding Shur mo Steam enabling of a piece of nutter-tubing on the end of pin is here. The nutter is split half way to release tail, a little grease put inside. It seems a cheap + very useful instrument. Can be obtained on indent. Divisional Scheme for returning Officers. Remarks on clipping and General Clipping Machines. Stated that its strong bits there have mechanical clippers — Infantry Brigade, 3 Field Ambulances, 3 Field Company R.E.! All communications to be in memorandum form.	

WAR DIARY or INTELLIGENCE SUMMARY

Army Form C. 2118

Place	Date	Hour	Summary of Events and Information	Remarks and references to Appendices
CAMBLAIN L'ABBÉ	9/10/16		No 522 (How) Battery arrived, also No 74 Sec LASSEY- T.C., A.T.C. now attached to 108/Bde - R.F.A. DDVS. and DDR Field Army inspected units of the Divisional Artillery at	
"	10/10/16		Visited 36 M.V.S., inspected their equipment, and 194 Cy A.T.C.	
"	11/10/16		Visited 72, 73, 74 Field Ambulances. The strength arrived at Divisional Artillery has been executed for detail, totals:- 108 Bde R.F.A. 45 Horses. 107 " " 55 " 108 " " 63 " (Lui) 109 " " 15 " D.A.C. " " 24 " Antiaircraft " " 2 " Left Division " " 1/2 " Total 203 1/2 / 220.	

WAR DIARY
INTELLIGENCE SUMMARY

Army Form C. 2118

Place	Date	Hour	Summary of Events and Information	Remarks and references to Appendices
CAMBLAIN L'ABBÉ	12/10/16		A.D.v.S. went on leave. Reported departure to D.D.v.S. First Army. Capt. J. Harris A.v.C. O.C. 36th V. Section answered for me. Kept in touch as regards studs. Studs' instructions from him. Wire received from D.D.v.S. First Army stating arrival of 107 Bde R.F.A. and re-acted to Mallem of a Bde veterinary hospital. Orders to Mallem Purdue of 107 Bde R.F.A. a/c	
"	13/10/16		Lieut Penny arrived. Was executed by 36th V.S. — So arrival from 24 Divisional Artillery and 7 from the unit. Mallemaing 8/107 Bde R.F.A. commenced — D.D.v.S. First Army notified a/c	
"	14/10/16		24 Division transferred from IV to XVII Corps. Mallemaing 107 Bde R.F.A. a/c	
"	15/10/16		Mallemaing 107 Bde R.F.A. a/c	

Army Form C. 2118

WAR DIARY
or
INTELLIGENCE SUMMARY
(Erase heading not required.)

Instructions regarding War Diaries and Intelligence Summaries are contained in F.S. Regs., Part II. and the Staff Manual respectively. Title Pages will be prepared in manuscript.

Place	Date	Hour	Summary of Events and Information	Remarks and references to Appendices
CAMBLAIN L'ABBÉ	16/10/16		The following arrived incorporated by 36th V. Section 78. Arrivals from 2nd Divisional Artillery, 2 from the units relieving 107 Bde. R.F.A. at ―	
"	17/10/16		Relieving 107 Bde. R.F.A. at ―	
"	18/10/16		Relieving arrival of 522 (How.) Bat. R.F.A.	
"	19/10/16		Reported to ADVS Fivth Army that at arrival of 107 Bde R.F.A. relieving with a negative result; also that of 522 (How) Battery R.F.A. at ―	
"	20/10/16		Applied for 155 draw horses to keep up 100 draw of 36th V. Section at ―	
"	21/10/16		ADVS. returned from leave – arrived Boulogne at 6.30 p.m. A.F.W. 3000 forwarded to DDVS. Fivth Army. at ―	

Army Form C. 2118

WAR DIARY
or
INTELLIGENCE SUMMARY
(Erase heading not required.)

Instructions regarding War Diaries and Intelligence Summaries are contained in F. S. Regs., Part II. and the Staff Manual respectively. Title Pages will be prepared in manuscript.

Place	Date	Hour	Summary of Events and Information	Remarks and references to Appendices
CAMBLAIN L'ABBÉ	22/10/16		Reported return from leave to ADMS First Army. 3 O.R. U.S. awaited returning animals — 43. 2nd Divisional Artillery and 6 from other units.	
"	23/10/16		Visited 33rd Bn Royal Fusiliers (Eatons) and 106 Bde R.F.A. at	
"	24/10/16		Visited 108 Bde R.F.A and 36 M.V. Section at Visited the D.M.C and Mrs Stansbury's 6/1/07 Bde R.F.A at GOUY SERVINS. Visited detachment J Mules (?) of Mob Sect. Vet DAC at ECOIVRES. Found animals in excellent condition, he awarded has finished hats due to military trucks running against them, due to ignorance or carelessness on part of drivers. at	
"	25/10/16		Visited horses at BRAQUEMONT — saw ADVS 40' Division, also ADVS 1st Canadian Division, arranged some of Mobile Veterinary Section to DAMBLAIN D ROUVIN. at	

Army Form C. 2118

WAR DIARY
or
INTELLIGENCE SUMMARY
(Erase heading not required.)

Place	Date	Hour	Summary of Events and Information	Remarks and references to Appendices
CAMBLAIN L'ABBÉ	26/10/16		Visited 106 Brigade R.F.A. Found 2 suspicious cases of mange sent to 36th V.S. for examination and report. Instructed D.D.V.C. to interpret at Hermonville gear. Clipr dues needed and isolate. Visited 36th V.S. and selected animals for inoculation. Visited No 2. Reserve Park in connection with a number of cases of colic. This is attributed to mules recommend changing train as had at present in use is contaminated. Suggest pieces from troughs. Selected piece for putting up new troughs. a.b	
"	27/10/16		Held conference of Veterinary Officers. Instructions given regarding inoculation of R.A. animals while attached to 1st Canadian Division. D.O. responsibility in regard to clipping order. Orders to see that every animal has a straphull or nosebag. Cases of injuries or sicker up and to be sent. Visited sick. Remaining Veterinary officer attaches there to D.D.V.S. First Army — Capt T. McDonell. 1st Canadian Division. Returned through A.F.A. 2000. a.b	
BRAY	28/10/16		Moved to BRAY, also 36th V. Section a.b	

WAR DIARY
or
INTELLIGENCE SUMMARY

(Erase heading not required.)

Army Form C. 2118

Place	Date	Hour	Summary of Events and Information	Remarks and references to Appendices
BRAY	29/10/16		Had 203 Remounts at Bruay Station for 2nd "Divisional Artillery. D.D.R. First Army was this day. Arrived divers cifn Spieces shipment and sent hues and one a 5m miles here from is Condition. at	
BRAQUEMONT	30/10/16 31/10/16		Arrived BRAQUEMONT and 2 btn. Y. Section moved to DROUVIN. Re: ADVS. 40 Division took no unih left behind. at Juice 3 bt. v.t.S. Interviewed the sluth gran Section with arrive. It then being exchanged for younger men from Base Veterinary Hospitals. Visited 19 Brigade Remuneration replacing clipping. TO attended reported at this office. Lt. Parker. A.V.C. called with aspect at these movement farmale office. Remounts Headquarters Division AD.V.S First Army. Visited 19 - Coy. ASC also been seen Mahipman belonging to 37 Siege Bath R.G.A. reports that Companions gave instructions to isolation Mannes. at	

CONFIDENTIAL.

Vol 15

WAR. DIARY.

of.

A.D.V.S. 24th Division.

FROM. 1-11-16. To. 30.11.16.
Vol. (15)

No. V1914
Date 1-12-16

WAR DIARY or INTELLIGENCE SUMMARY

Army Form C. 2118

ADVS - 24th Division

Place	Date	Hour	Summary of Events and Information	Remarks and references to Appendices
BRAQUEMONT	1/11/16		Inspected War Diary (W.D. W) Base and Depôt etc Corps & 17th Division (W.D. 10-14 inclusive) of O/c Remts. A.V.C. Hotlinck. Visited 188 & park of 181 and 178 Bde R.F.A. 40th Division attached to Division. Visited H.Q. Company 40 Divl. Train, 191 & 197 Companies A.S.C. Train. Found several animals clipped nr & saddle patchs left. Written instructions to 40 Division in writing. Lunched with G.O.C. Division - discussed matters connected with Divl. Mobile Veterinary Section, clipping.	at
"	2/11/16		Visited Nos 1. 2. 3 M.V. Section 4th Reserve Park. Drawn up Routine Orders - contained instructions as regards clipping - New Order for all drivers of horses or vehicles, during winter months, animals happening to be killed to any length of time.	at 4th Reserve Park.
"	3/11/16		Weekly conference of Veterinary Officers representative of F.A. 2000.	
"	4/11/16		Accompanied D.D.V.S First Army on inspection of 4th Reserve Park (H.Qrs. No 1. 2 & 3 Sections) M.V. Food Orderlies. Picketed No 2 Section.	

WAR DIARY
INTELLIGENCE SUMMARY

Army Form C. 2118

Place	Date	Hour	Summary of Events and Information	Remarks and references to Appendices
BRAQUEMONT	4/7/16 (cont'd)		No 2 Section. Oran h.o.H.D. and C.O's. his riding horse had been clipped throughout, certain h.Q/A.Q. orders held, interview with O.C. Division and A.D. M.S. remarks on reduction of horse recently brought catton out.	
"	5/7/16		Conference of A.D.'s V.S. at Offices of D.D.V.S. First Army. Remarks on preparation of A.F. A 2000 - particulars as regards Column "Remaining" what action when units are transferred to other Formation. In some Armies there are attached to other divisions — Chairman "Transferred Sick". D.D.V.S. First Army does not them stand at all — asked for a ruling on the matter. Regimen was discussed without opening up held it did not exhibit much evidence of contagion in this country (France), further informed that Itchy mange was to reckoned r Skin used under Mange of no difference. Ration of Hay is not to Thanes :— L.D. 6 Hay, 4 Straw. H.D. 6 Hay, 7 Straw. So horse ration is reduced all round L.D.by 2 lb and H.D. 4 lb. One O/Chief-certain French-Scotch to be approved. Procedure in discovering Mange among Civil animals. Report Owners Name address to A.P.M. Formation. No inhuman killing instinct can be carried out by British Army. Found two sick but animal skip kept have stalls until cured — apparently failing civil machines - this responsibility falls on A.V. Carps.	

WAR DIARY
INTELLIGENCE SUMMARY

Army Form C. 2118

Place	Date	Hour	Summary of Events and Information	Remarks and references to Appendices
BRAQUE MONT	5/7/16		A.V.C.S. Returned a case of suspected sarcin[?] proving a singeing tramp move from trench to modern. at	
"	6/7/16		Visits 73rd Infantry Brigade and Machine Gun Company and 1st Royal Fusiliers and 255th Tunnelling Coy R.E. + 3 Ch.N.S. at	
"	7/7/16		Pte No S4/18479 Travett. W.R. A.S.C. arrived to relieve P. Kenington who is being transferred to Infantry.	
"	7/7/16		Visits 40 D.A.C. (1, 2, 3 Section) Animals here generally in good condition. No 1 + 3 Section being very good. Newly-arrived animals had their clog trimmed and No 3 Section. At these new appliques face high (Reported to H.Q. 40 Divisional Artillery) at	
"	8/7/16		Visits No 181 and 188 Brigade R.F.A. 40 Division. Found no here to gort condition. Sent 1-3 H[ors]es from C/181 to M.V. Sep[?] Veterinary Hospital. In cultus case here had been trimming Shell C/181 which had no refreshing approache at back in fed healthy.	

WAR DIARY
or
INTELLIGENCE SUMMARY

Army Form C. 2118

(Erase heading not required.)

Place	Date	Hour	Summary of Events and Information	Remarks and references to Appendices
BRAQUEMONT	11/9/16		H.R.H. Duke of CONNAUGHT visited Divisional Area inspected certain units. Visited GAUCHIN LEGAL and saw No 3 Company 24th Divisional Train.	
"	11/10/16		Healthy exposure Mulvenany. Officers preparation of A.F. A 2000. Visited 36th mile returning Section.	
"	11/11/16		Interviews with G.O.C. Division. Visited 178th R.F.A. and H.Q. Company, 40th Divisional Train in Tincelin with some cases of Necrosis.	
"	11/13/16		Accompanied D.D.R. First Army when inspecting animal Coat for the ham Veterinary Reserve. Visited No 4 Section 40° D.A.C at HESDIGNEUIL, 36th I. Section	
"	11/14/16		Accompanied DDVS, and DDR First Army who inspected 40° Divisional Artillery and DAC. Took me car of superior Horse at No 2 Section 40 D.A.C & sent same to 36 M.V.S. preparation.	
"	11/15/16		Visited 36 M.V. Section. Arrival of 34° D.F. Signal Company. 24 Divisional Train.	

WAR DIARY
or
INTELLIGENCE SUMMARY

(Erase heading not required.)

Army Form C. 2118

Place	Date	Hour	Summary of Events and Information	Remarks and references to Appendices
BRAQUEMONT.	16-11-16		Visited No 3 Company A.S.C. & 40' D.A.C. (3 Section) at	
"	17-11-16		Weekly conference of Veterinary Officers. Inspected M.F. Horse. Sgt. BETHEL M.C. Transferred from 3 Bns. to 2 B Bde R.F.A. 5 Division	
"	18-11-16		Visited 3 Bde. V. Section. Reexamined with G.O.C. Division at	
"	19-11-16		Visited 17 Infantry Brigade & examined 1st Royal Fusiliers Animals who had acne. Mange. at	
"	20-11-16		Visited 3 Bde. V. Section and 31st (A.T.) Company R.E. at MINX. also 40 D.A.C.	
"	21-11-16		Visited 187 and 188 Bde R.F.A. new arrangement for actual shoeing saw animal with Tin Foils. Present animals picking up nails. at	
"	22-11-16		Visited 36 M.F.S. and went to BARLIN to see A.D.V.S. 2 Canadian Division regarding evacuation from D/108.Bde R.F.A. at	
"	23-11-16		Went to HERSIN and inspected D/108 Bde R.F.A.	

Army Form C. 2118

WAR DIARY
or
INTELLIGENCE SUMMARY
(Erase heading not required.)

Instructions regarding War Diaries and Intelligence Summaries are contained in F.S. Regs., Part II. and the Staff Manual respectively. Title Pages will be prepared in manuscript.

Place	Date	Hour	Summary of Events and Information	Remarks and references to Appendices
BRAQUEMONT	24.11.16		Weekly Conference of returning Officers for punctuation D.A.D.V.S.	
	25.11.16		Weekly interview with GOC Division. Detached visits of one Officer (Cpl LAURIE Attd.) and six non STBM V.S. proceeded to RELY to receive from 39' and 25 Divisional Artillery proving their work areas of 1st Army.	
	26.11.16		Visited Slaughterer - 936 cups at RELY. Saw Brynice Major 1st Div. Arlillery regarding innoculation of Horses. at	
	27.11.16		Visited Farriers Shop of A.V.C. with reference to claim of card to shoeing hand - have shoes from stores - Advisory form unavailable as I do not have enough heat - is effectively held. Ordered O.C. Divisional Train to issue Coffee a Smith and for that purpose. Visited 36 cups . 187 Bde R.F.A. with effect of his plate Pfeuen- poilin April. at	
	28.11.16		Visits 40(D.AC) 140 Section . and 158 Bde R.F.A. at	

WAR DIARY
INTELLIGENCE SUMMARY

Army Form C. 2118

Place	Date	Hour	Summary of Events and Information	Remarks and references to Appendices
BRAQUEMONT	29.11.16		Visited No 3 Section 40 D.A.C. Have animals & mules ago have been dutiful well cared. Since the reduction of troops they are beginning to pull up. Visited 36th M Section.	
	30.11.16		Visited animals of Field Ambulances. Sent reserve a letter. 6 M.S. Prevention of Mildli. Visited 3 Bring team animals. Checked from 39 & 25 Divisional Artillery.	

CONFIDENTIAL.

Vol 16

WAR DIARY.
of
A·D·V·S.
24th DIVISION.

FROM. 1-12-16. TO. 31-12-16.

VOL. 16.

WAR DIARY
or
INTELLIGENCE SUMMARY

Army Form C. 2118

ADVS
24th Division

(Erase heading not required.)

Place	Date	Hour	Summary of Events and Information	Remarks and references to Appendices
BRAQUEMONT	1-12-16		Held Conference Veterinary Officers. Inspection of A.T. Stores. Inspected 4 Cobs and 1 Mule of 24 Signal Company & transfer to Advanced Remount Depôt at GONNE HEM. Inspected 24 H.D. Horse of 2nd Reserve Park attached to 24 Division. Transferred War Diary for November to A.D.G.'s Office at 1st Base. a.L.	
"	2-12-16		Visited No 4 Section 40 "D.A.C at HESDIGNEUL. 36 m.v. Section. a.L	
"	3-12-16		Visited M.B. Towell. Ave. 70 % 106 Brigade R.F.A arrived at Office. 40 Divisional Artillery commenced Transfer. a.L	
"	4-12-16		24th Divisional Artillery arrived. Visited Brigades on the march, also 9 & 40". Divisional Artillery marching out. Visited 36 m.v. Section. a.L	

WAR DIARY
INTELLIGENCE SUMMARY

Army Form C. 2118

Place	Date	Hour	Summary of Events and Information	Remarks and references to Appendices
BRAQUEMONT	5.12.16		Inspected animals of 188 Brigade R.F.A. with V.O. 9/c. A.D.S Batteries had improved. 9cwr suspicious mange cases from C/Batty. C/D/Batts. only have mange. Line Officer told new regiment as regards clipping. ct	
"	6.12.16		Conference of A.D.V.S. at office of D.D.V.S. First Army. Subjects discussed. Returns (Remit of Animal Management & Divisional Schools during the winter months. Progress effect of refuse from Beef Distilleries and amounting hutts. It was for Animals. Employer acidophlint. Current Chop prices. Horse deaths, at Bruay and La Bourse. Conspicuous Returns & instructions to M.O's. One Officer (Capt. J. M. Zaurée - Acc) has been proceeded to Monchy Breton with the ambulance to check animals from 40 Divisional. Atkins marching out of First Army Back Area. Proceeded to Monchy Breton and arranged with Staff Captain 40" Division Atkins regarding rail & Autos of M.V Section detachment. Issued order to R.A. Brigade setting position of M.V.S. Gave list of Billets to O.C. 3 Btrs. who met First Army Atkins any animals unable to march. cb	

WAR DIARY
or
INTELLIGENCE SUMMARY

(Erase heading not required.)

Army Form C. 2118

Place	Date	Hour	Summary of Events and Information	Remarks and references to Appendices
BRAQUEMONT	7.12.16		Visits by D.A.C with V.O. %c (Capt. J. Blackburn arr.) - A/107 and A/107 ant Neux Les Mines Station. 10w Remarks arrive. Met D.D.V.S. Field Army. Visited MAZINGARBE and saw a M.M.P. Horse opposite with Azoturia. Visited LES BREBIS and saw new Horse standards thrown at 8th War Rents. 9th EAST SURREYS, 1st and 12th Royal Fusiliers, 8th Butts. V.O. %c not present.	ab
"	8.12.16		Weekly conference of Veterinary Officers and Inspection of A.F. A 2076. Discussed Official Correspondence - Sick of animals for October. Routine tendering with Care of Supplies etc. Scenery - charge Dress - Cattle Office. 18 CRW Lt 36th. V.S. Transmission of Patients. Capt. F.W. TRYDELL M.C. absent. Temporarily SICK.	ab
"	9.12.16		Visits by D.A.C at 17 CHOKIN and HESDIGNEUL. Inspected animal with C.O. and V.O. %c. No.1 Section has trouble. No.2 Train had new Cavalier - No.3 Train and No.4 Sect. having new Officer to each section. Detachment +No.30th V Section returned evening of 8.12.16.	ab

WAR DIARY

INTELLIGENCE SUMMARY

(Erase heading not required.)

Army Form C. 2118

Place	Date	Hour	Summary of Events and Information	Remarks and references to Appendices
BRAQUEMONT	10/12/16		Visited 107 Brigade R.F.A. (A.B.C. Batteries). Inspection of Amn. Column A. Fair. B. good - C. Improving. Visited C/110 Bde. R.F.A who've had 14 cases of fever. Ito be have returned, and four cases of suspicious splenic at D/106. (2 remounts and 2 old animals) Serviceability of 3 6-pdrs prevailed; permission for an 2 old animals, which had be evacuated at it.	
"	11-12-16		Visited 108 Bde R.F.A. A.B.C Batteries are improving. In good Inspection of Ammunition Column. Officers mess present, at and interior Magazine lines. Visited D/107 Bde R.F.A. - No major line present. Creation fair. Issued instructions to Veterinary Officer regarding Medical lectures on Animal Management to be submitted by hours. Saw A.A. Anh Division regarding Intelligence of Chaffeukens.	
"	12.12.16		Inspected animals of 73 Infantry Brigade with Brigade Commander. All animals are in good condition but shoeing of 73rd Machine Gun Company, and 2nd Kendal Reg't. requires attention. reported to be 1.0% on the matter. C.L.	

Army Form C. 2118

WAR DIARY
~~INTELLIGENCE SUMMARY~~
(Erase heading not required.)

Instructions regarding War Diaries and Intelligence Summaries are contained in F.S. Regs., Part II. and the Staff Manual respectively. Title Pages will be prepared in manuscript.

Place	Date	Hour	Summary of Events and Information	Remarks and references to Appendices
BRAQUEMONT	13.12.16		Interviewed C.R.A. Division with reference to Autumn Horses remarks on horses. Line Officers and Clipping Mules. Visited 36A V.S. & attached animals to evacuation. Visited C/106 Brigade R.F.A. and gave Course improving some returns. Totals:- Visited Transport lines of 1st & 12th Royal Fusiliers. 73 Machine Gun Company. 8th and Kenfig. of East Surreys. Shewed Farriers No 3 Field Company R.E. at Rushpits. a/L	
"	14.12.16		Visited Divisional Technical School afternoon giving lecture on Animal Management With Classes, also SeaDick Captain R.E. on some subject with regard to the Schl. Visited 36th V.C. a/L	
"	15.12.16		Heavy conference M.O. preparation T.A.F.A 2000. Remarks on Syllabus of lectures, arrangements to be made. Visited 10th Middlesex R.F.A with Staff Captain R.E. to inspect animals from lines. a/L	
"	16.12.16		Interviewed with O.C. Visited C/106 Brigade R.F.A a/L	

Place	Date	Hour	Summary of Events and Information	Remarks and references to Appendices
BRAQUEMONT	17.12.16		Received instructions from DDVS, Third Army, to take returning Horses & Mules to "Q" Reserve Park just arrived from SOMME operations. Visited HESDIGNEUL - inspected 358 animals of 9 "Q" Reserve Park. All stores except ffulage were generally in upon condition. 31 FB Horse were left arrived in 3rd Army here and are in Third Army lines. Reported A.F.A. some, reported to DDVS, Third Army. Detailed Cpt. J. BLACKBURN, AVC to assume veterinary duties, informed CO that the position of 36 M.V.S. terminal new shipped. Arrived shippings animals to rest out-in their section block. as they are very crowded + remounts are in the open. Arranged inspection for returning states. Visited 191 Machine Gun Company just arrived from several. Animals in good Condition - horse clipped + sheing requires attention. Skin M. 13 Horse 47 Mules. Detailed Cpt. TRYDELL AVC on V.O.% whose unit is at its present billet at	
"	18.12.16		Visited Pherinighwich :- 10G, D/106, B/107, Brigade R.F.A., 196 Bg aif 3rd Australian Travelling Company.	

WAR DIARY
INTELLIGENCE SUMMARY

Army Form C. 2118

Place	Date	Hour	Summary of Events and Information	Remarks and references to Appendices
BRAQUEMONT	19.12.16		Inspected at the animals of 9' Reserve Park. Sent Ptes Morris, b. 3 Blunt 3 H.S. Mathks, S.T.R. to V.Cii examination. (One found little affected with Sarcoptic Mange) at	
"	20.12.16		Visited 195 & 197 Coys A.S.C. all sickness. 9' Reserve Park. Visited animals of 24 Divisional Training Batn. at ALLOUAGNE. Visited D.D.V.S. First Army at LILLERS. L.S.H.B.L.S. A.V.C. 70 % 1st Corps Cavalry Rgt. visited by D.D.V.S. First Army in 70 % 9' Reserve Park at	
"	21.12.16		Visited 36 Ambulance selected animals for examination at	
"	22.12.16		V.O's Conference preparation of A.F. a 2000. at	
"	23.12.16		Inspected individually every animal in Coy 100 Beer R. M. 9 Horses sent to 36 M.V.S. for examination (mange). Visited 36 M.V.S. examined Scurvying & 6 Horses visited. returned with Sd. Cn. Sophies returned Grimil. Visited A.A. Coy R.F.A. Coy R.A. re mange. at	

WAR DIARY
or
INTELLIGENCE SUMMARY

Army Form C. 2118

Place	Date	Hour	Summary of Events and Information	Remarks and references to Appendices
BEAUMONT	24-12-16		Notice received of A.D.S.'s Divisional Train and R.E. Divisional order published regarding Mange. D.R.O. 1991. dated 24-12-16 state :— Army 15th Intelligence MANGE :— 1. All animals Transferred from one unit to another must previously be inspected by a V.O. 2. Transfer from infected units is forbidden (see G.R.O. 441) 3. Animals found shown to be infected, or examined by a V.O. as soon as possible. All Animals Transferred from the Division will be inspected by the A.D.V.S. his applies to animals transferred to other Divisions, to Remount Depôts or Field Remount Section. (see D.R.O. 1988) 5. Remounts should be isolated for 10 days on joining. at	
"	25-12-16		Visited 36 M.V.S. at	
"	26-12-16		Visited B and C Batteries 106 Bde R.F.A. - D/108 - B/107. at	
"	27-12-16		Visited No 3 Section Reserve Park. 73. Infantry Brigade. at	

WAR DIARY

Army Form C. 2118

Place: BEAUQUESNE

Date	Hour	Summary of Events and Information
28.10.16		Visits Nors Company & Divisional Train - 36 in Train. No 3 Section Reinforced.
29.10.16		Held Conference Veterinary Officers. Inspected Sp. of A. dump. Visited M.A.2 in CARD E as inspected 191 Machine Gun Company. Orders of arrival fair. Shoeing very bad - Horse hot fitted and feet very worn & not prepared for shoe. Horses & Shoes M.E. & Horse Arranges for Competent Sgt and S.S. to take off wire & rehire herses. Sgt. Smith - also from A.S.C. Transport Sergeant Reported on actin D.V.O.C. Division. a/f
30.10.16		There are 17 Cases of pickers opened during Period ending 28" inst: have special report to G.O.C. Division and D.D.V.S. First Army. 13 will have pickers up in the Breks - due to having been without attention through Picarely. Horses in the rear. health inform with G.O.C Division Practice Gas alarm. hd 1st Cavalry Brigade R. E. Squadron at Neuve le MINES Stables at 8 pm.
31.10.16		Visited 1st Cavalry Brigade M.G. Squadron - Four wheel cranked running shoeing. Outstirs fair. Visited 17 & 72 Infantry Brigades. a/f

36 © luth: Feb: Sect:
tot: 5

CONFIDENTIAL.

Vol 17

WAR DIARY

of

A.D.V.S

24th DIVISION.

From 1-1-17 To 31-1-17.

Vol. 17.

WAR DIARY
or
INTELLIGENCE SUMMARY ADVS. 24th DIVISION.

(Erase heading not required.)

Army Form C. 2118

Place	Date	Hour	Summary of Events and Information	Remarks and references to Appendices
BRAQUEMONT	1-1-17		1st Cavalry Machine Gun Squadron arrived. Inspected animals. Cartier Farm - Sheing arrangt. Visited 191 Machine Gun Company. Improving animals on hind shoe up. Visited C/108 and D/107 Bde R.F.A. and 36th V.S. a/v	
"	2-1-17		Visited 24 D.A.C. Examined animals in No 3. Section - u MAN O.E. Examined every animal in B/108 Bde R.F.A. Sent in 3 Horses for examination/escaping at 36th V.S. Found two officers Clarges Clippers turifoul. a/v	
"	3-1-17		Visited No 4. Sect - 24 D.A.C. Sent in 2 cases Surgifice Skin fr examination at 36th V. Section. Sent Vet Cpl. R.A. rejoining B/108 - 4 Sect 24 D.A.C. a/v	
"	4-1-17		Visited 36th V.S. and 72 Infantry Brigade. a/v	

WAR DIARY
INTELLIGENCE SUMMARY

Army Form C. 2118

Place	Date	Hour	Summary of Events and Information	Remarks and references to Appendices
BEAUMONT	5.1.17		Inspected animals of D.T.M.B. HQrs R.A. & R.E. Weekly Conference Veterinary Officers preparing M.F. A2000. Remounts arrange necessary training all others of itchy animals. Drew attention to the orders against dumping of Droppings & Circular Capt. J. Blackburn are proceed on leave to England.	
"	6.1.17		Weekly interview with L.O.C. Division – reports on P.V.N. Machine Gun Companies – clipping of legs & heels.	
"	7.1.17		Attended C.R.A. much rain whole week, return horses dries – manges – values & clipping men – Ord. L 107 Bde – due to not putting down sufficient chalk not slag. Visits C/106, B/106, C/107 Bars R.A. head to All Organise and an 12 Junior from Cavalry Reserve Rgmts (5 Lancers & 12 Lancers) – Informed there been on regards shoeing – Veterinary duties – att.	

WAR DIARY
or
INTELLIGENCE SUMMARY

Army Form C. 2118

Place	Date	Hour	Summary of Events and Information	Remarks and references to Appendices
BRAQUEMONT	8.1.17		Visited 3rd Divn. S. Base Dep. R.A. &c	
"	9.1.17		Inspection due to frost. &c	
"	10.1.17		Visited 3 Dn. V. Section - M.M.P. Horses. One Officer Chief Officer. Held enquiry re Lieut. J.R. BARKER A.V.C. Inspected Remount A-C/106 and A/106 Brigade R.F.A. &c	
"	11.1.17		Visited 191 Machine Gun Company, 3rd Cavalry Pioneer Bn., 1 M. Tank, 2nd D.A.C. (No 3 Section) and 3 Dn. V. Section &c	
"	12.1.17		Held Conference of Veterinary Officers. Preparation S.A.F.M. 2000. &c	
"	13.1.17		Visited 3 Dn. V. Section, heavy Wonen. G.O.C. Divn. C.R.A. A.A. and Q.G. Divn. &c	

Army Form C. 2118

WAR DIARY
or
INTELLIGENCE SUMMARY
(Erase heading not required.)

Place	Date	Hour	Summary of Events and Information	Remarks and references to Appendices
BRAQUEMONT	14.1.17		Monthly Conference of A.D.M.S. at First Army H.Qrs. The following matters were discussed:— 1. Re-organization of Motor Ambulance affecting Volunteer Personnel in Divisions. 2. Inspection abolishing the O.C. M.V. Section. General opinion was that it had effect the Section, not to enhance T officers(?), in our opinion a smoother running on any big scale would affect its efficiency. The Division Service. It was agreed that an Officer should live at the H.V.S. – to whose units as well as being O.C. of Section. 3. Appointment of A.D.M.S. to Corps. 4. Formation of Corps M.V. Section from Divisional M.V. Sections bring(?) 1 NCO & 3 men from each Section. 5. The following diseases are discovered. Measles, Mumps, Ger(?) Catarrhal(?), Flu, Tub.(?) 6. Stopping Beetles for Prevention of other diseases.	

Army Form C. 2118

WAR DIARY
or
INTELLIGENCE SUMMARY
(Erase heading not required.)

Instructions regarding War Diaries and Intelligence Summaries are contained in F.S. Regs., Part II. and the Staff Manual respectively. Title Pages will be prepared in manuscript.

Place	Date	Hour	Summary of Events and Information	Remarks and references to Appendices
Bracquemont	15-1-17		Visited 36th V.S. – M.M.P. R.A.M.C. – No 3 Sect. 9 Reserve Park.	
"	16-1-17		Hutchison Lecture from 21st Division arrived & was attached – C94 – C96 – Sgt. Inspected teeth married. Visited 72. Machine Gun Company, at	
"	17-1-17		Visited 36th V Section and C/108th Bde R.F.A. at	
"	18-1-17		Visited 96 Brigade – 3 Australian Tunnelling Company, at	
"	19-1-17		Medical Conference of Veterinary officers. Stomatitis Battalion Catapren Ordered out to A/106 and C/107 Brigades R.F.A. South addresses of Conference have since rendered at 12 Noon till Conference of A.D.V.S. Dec 14th host - at	
"	20-1-17		Visited 36 M V Section – C/106 – D/106 – Staff Capt D.R. at Interview with D.O.C. Division M.D. S M.D. g Staff Capt D.R. at	

WAR DIARY
or
INTELLIGENCE SUMMARY

Army Form C. 2118

(Erase heading not required.)

Place	Date	Hour	Summary of Events and Information	Remarks and references to Appendices
BRAQUEMONT	21-1-17		Visited 19 Cy. A.S.C. - 3 Sect. 9 Reserve Park. A.D.S. 2nd Division. Had Amn. & hand round Pool of Area. Arranged with Staff Capt. R.A. regarding inspection of Divisional Artillery by D.D.V.S. Final Army on 24-1-17 at.	
"	22-1-17		Infantry. & D.D.V.S. Visit - Vet. & Shoeing features see miles:- A.B.C.D. 106. Bde R.F.A. A.C. 1107 Bde R.F.A. H.Q. 108 Bde R.F.A. at	
"	23-1-17		Visited B.D./107 Bde R.F.A. C.D./108 Bde R.F.A. and 36 bde V. Section at Section 1-2-3-24-24. D.A.C.	
"	24-1-17		D.D.V.S. Final Army his visits see Divisional Artillery at	
"	25-1-17		Visited Philosophe to attend a Court of Inquiry on the transport Officer of 72-17. Sby. Gave evidence regarding condition & care of transport animals. Visited S.Capt R.A. reference re-organization of Artillery. at	

WAR DIARY
or
INTELLIGENCE SUMMARY
(Erase heading not required.)

Army Form C. 2118

Place	Date	Hour	Summary of Events and Information	Remarks and references to Appendices
BRAQUEMONT	26-1-17		Monthly Conferences of Veterinary Officers. Preparation of A.F. A 2000. Gave D.D.'s instruction returning from J Division H. Rest Area. Arrived Hospital Funnel & Communication with me on his arrival in that.	at
"	27-1-17		Health inspection with S.O.C. A.A.Q.M.G, Staff Capt. R.A. horses A/106 - A/107 Brigade R.F.A. - 73 Res. Ambulance.	at
"	28-1-17		Visited Div. Divisional Train, 3 C.A. & Section.	at
"	29-1-17		Visits Subject Company. A.B/108, APRC /106 - A/107 Brigade R.F.A.	at
"	30-1-17 } 31-1-17 }		In Piert Kerkhlane. Care to effect from tune from a fire.	at

Confidential.

Vol 18

War Diary.

of

A.D.V.S.

24th Division.

From. 1-2-17. To. 28-2-17.

Vol. 18.

WAR DIARY or INTELLIGENCE SUMMARY

A.D.V.S. 24th Division

Army Form C. 2118

Place	Date	Hour	Summary of Events and Information	Remarks and references to Appendices
BRAQUEMONT	1.2.17		Sick in Field ambulance. at	
	2.2.17		Returned to duty. Office. heads Conference DO's preparation of AFA 2010. at	
	3.2.17		Interview G.O.C. Division. ADC aq.g. Asst for to Office at J.O.L	
	4.2.17		Horses available. Proceed to 1st Army N. Qrs. for monthly Conference of ADsVs. Phase DDVS. 1st Army for that effect. at	
	5.2.17		Proceeded on leave from 5-15 incl. to England. Capt. J.H. LAURIE. AVC. O.C. 36 M.V.S. Tomorrow to me. Left orders in writing as to duties also preliminary arrangements to case division moves during absence. Report to DDVS. relieving ADVS. All Transport of duties to Veterinary Officer. at	
	6.2.17		The following extras up to 15 & including 16: not are from information supplied by Capt. J.H. LAURIE A.V.C. who was answering for me:— Capt. J.H. LAURIE A.V.C. visited 2.30 p.m. horses mobilization to V.O: reference arrivals and to Butcher. at	

WAR DIARY
or
INTELLIGENCE SUMMARY

(Erase heading not required.)

Army Form C. 2118

Place	Date	Hour	Summary of Events and Information	Remarks and references to Appendices
BRAQUEMONT	7.2.17		Capt. Laurie - called. Read out copies of 1st Corps held on Animal Management Topo's at	
	8.2.17		Capt Laurie called. Compare times from D.Officer references ADVS inspecting 27 Surplus Horses of 6th Division & 16 of 24th Division - to be sent to No.1. Field Remount Section - Gonnehem - Arrangements. The nurse with C.R.A. Capt LAURIE inspected 7 Horses D/106, & 8 of D/107. 4 three of the number inspected sent to 36 M.V.S. a Veterinary Case, & remainder certified fit to proceed to No. 1. Field Remount Section. at	
	9.2.17		Capt LAURIE called 9.30 am, visited C.R.A. D.O. afterwards with newly returns at 10 a.m. Newly stated times F.D.D.S. 1st Army. Scout conference re - move of Division received from "G" at	
	10.2.17		Capt. Laurie called at 10 am & 3-pm. - ADVS 37 Division called. Made arrangement re move of 36 M.V.S. to units & ADVS. 37 Division - List of Units to administer in Area. Copies of A.F.A 2006 - Mai 9 Batts etc - also	

WAR DIARY
or
INTELLIGENCE SUMMARY
(Erase heading not required.)

Army Form C. 2118

Place	Date	Hour	Summary of Events and Information	Remarks and references to Appendices
BEAUMONT				
	10.2.17		(Cont'd) Trips of horses paraded & advised M.V.S. checking Inol. Formed meets A.F. A. A. arms & D.D.V.S. 1st Army. 1st Corps C.R.A, & Evacuated 40 others. V.O's o/c advised. Visit of To Braure dull when M.V.S. moved same. at	
	11-2.17		Capt. LAURIE called 9.30 AM. Have 3.5.0. Division in consequent of Supplies to M.V.S. during move. - Wired V.O's as me. J M.V.S. with Lieutin S. Same. Instructed him to visit A.D.V.S. at LA BRUVIÈRE at 10 am. Friday - a head at	
	12.2.17		Capt. LAURIE called 10 am. Passes Office preparation France. at	
LA BEUVRIÈRE	13.2.17		Moved to LA BEUVRIÈRE. at	
	14.2.17		Capt. LAURIE called noon. Visit DDVS. 1st Army. London J ADVS Office & M.V.S. VO's wished as to veterinary Charges. at	

WAR DIARY
INTELLIGENCE SUMMARY
(Erase heading not required.)

Army Form C. 2118

Place	Date	Hour	Summary of Events and Information	Remarks and references to Appendices
LABEUVRIÈRE	15.2.17		Cpl. Lawrie called - listening to report of	
	16.2.17		At T.O. applied at Office re 16" unit. A.F. A 2002 prepared - ADVS. (Major Leaning) returned from leave midnight of	
	17.2.17		Orig Euphenga did not go out but remained in Office all day. of	
	18.2.17		Same as 17" unit of	
	19.2.17		Visited ECORDEEQUES & saw 36 M.V.S. & 4/108 B & v.P. T.E. Inspected 3 horses for transfer from Divisional Training Batt to the units in Division - Capt. LAURIE A.V.C. proceeded on leave to ENGLAND from 19 - 1st March. Capt. T. BLACKBURN A.V.C. acting O.C. 36 b. v. Section. Attended his absence attending animals inpt French 134 Division at St HILAIRE. Visited ALLOUAGNE - 72 M.G. Co - 72 9.B Transport. of	

WAR DIARY
INTELLIGENCE SUMMARY

Army Form C. 2118

Place	Date	Hour	Summary of Events and Information	Remarks and references to Appendices
LABEUVRIÈRE.	20.2.17		Sent evacuating party from 36 K/S to St HILAIRE to check animals infit to proceed from 3rd Division. Motor Horse Ambulance also present. One M.O. of 41st Division in Train, at 41st D.A.C. animals from St HILAIRE Cases left on 9.11.16. at	
	21.2.17		Visited LAPUGNOY and ALLOUAGNE & inspected 191 Machine Gun Company. Transport 73 Infantry Brigade. 103 Field Company R.E. Visited ECQUEDECQUES and 36 k.v.S. inspected 19 Sick animals. 15 Evacuated and 2 to destruction rolling to Butcher. At month examined no evidence of Stomatitis. at	
	22.2.17		Visited ANNEZIN and D.v.C Baths 107th R.F.A. - FORONERENIL. part of 14th Infantry Brigade and 159 Field Company R.E. at	
	23.2.17		Monthly Conference of Veterinary Officers & preparation of A.F. A form. Inspect 73 Machine Gun Company - 73rd Infantry Brigade at	
	24.2.17		Visited Units at FORQUIERES and FORONERENIL. Ricci Marci St HILAIRE and R.E. at HAM. EN. ARTOIS. at	

WAR DIARY
or
INTELLIGENCE SUMMARY

(Erase heading not required.)

Army Form C. 2118

Place	Date	Hour	Summary of Events and Information	Remarks and references to Appendices
LABEUVRIERE	25.2.17		Visited ECQUEDECQUES D. A.C. 36 M.V.S. and 2A. at HAM-EN-ARTOIS.	
	26.2.17		Visited Companies of the Divisional Train & 1st Royal Fusiliers.	
	27.2.17		Visited 1st S. Pauli Bath and 107 Bde R.F.G.	
	28.2.17		Visited ADVS. 1st Canadian Division at BARLIN & got information regarding his area. Visited ECQUEDECQUES and 36 A.V.S. inspected and examined mules & pole animals for evacuation. 3 H.s retained for treatment.	

CONFIDENTIAL.

Vol 19

WAR. DIARY.

of

A.D.V.S.

24th DIVISION.

FROM. 1-3-19. TO. 31-3-19.

VOL. 19.

Army Form C. 2118.

WAR DIARY
or
INTELLIGENCE SUMMARY A.D.V.S. 24th DIVISION

(Erase heading not required.)

Instructions regarding War Diaries and Intelligence Summaries are contained in F.S. Regs., Part II. and the Staff Manual respectively. Title Pages will be prepared in manuscript.

Place	Date	Hour	Summary of Events and Information	Remarks and references to Appendices
LABEUVRIÈRE	1.3.17		Visited 72nd and 73rd Infantry Brigades.	
	2.3.17		Visited 107 Bde R.F.A. — 129 Field Company R.E. Horse of Reinforcement left with that Company affected with a starred fracture near knee, made arrangements for leaving animal until fit to move. Held conference of Veterinary Officers and Proprietors of A.F.A. 2000. Explained views of Division - fraction fluids.	
	3.3.17		Capt. I.H. LAURIE, A.V.C. returned from leave. Capt. J. BLACKBURN, A.V.C. returned to H.Qrs 24th D.A.C. Made arrangements to move of M.V.S.	
	4.3.17		Conference of AD'sVS at Office of DD.V.S. H.Qrs 1st Army. Subjects under discussion :- Shoeing. 1. Question the Cavalry with regard to offensive operations. A Established and utility of Advance Collecting Posts. General opinion that there are necessary, also to train places to facilitate for further advance, since to simulate for.	

WAR DIARY or INTELLIGENCE SUMMARY

Army Form C. 2118.

Place	Date	Hour	Summary of Events and Information	Remarks and references to Appendices
LABEUVRIÈRE	4.3.17		Advance.	

(a)(i) B. Pack Transport. Are special Saddles necessary, if not what is the best method of carrying ammunition & supplies.

1) For Ammunition. Canvas shells with pockets. Carry Field Artillery Shells. These can be slung over Universal riding Saddle.

2) For supplies. Maximum Pack Saddle necessary, or better his fitted with mules, is a frame to afford a hold or pack saddle. Carry 8 tins - approx weight 50 lbs.

3) Issue Method of carrying own rations. No saddle required. One his Saddle Blanket. Feeds are placed in animals back. Sack. Same size is used for carrying feed. These Sacks are nearly filled, tied i centre forming a nest or blanket is thrown position

— Three of these Sacks filled in place and secured by one rope in a special method.

(a) Water arrangement — Several small troughs in different places are preferable to a few large ones. Should be all on one side of rows & fenced to prevent crushing at troughs. Time Table as necessary & efficient control by Traffic Police.

Army Form C. 2118.

WAR DIARY
or
INTELLIGENCE SUMMARY
(Erase heading not required.)

Instructions regarding War Diaries and Intelligence Summaries are contained in F. S. Regs., Part II. and the Staff Manual respectively. Title Pages will be prepared in manuscript.

Place	Date	Hour	Summary of Events and Information	Remarks and references to Appendices
LABEUVRIÈRE	4.3.17	(A.M.)	Police. 1) Matters spoken of E. & D. pett. Present issue to proper manifestation. Aggravation - Solution: Expansion or plus stopper better. 2) Dipping Baths. General opinion necessary. 4) Necessity to advertising practice of M.M.s. Veterinary Section. 5) Inspection of pamphlets have before return to Field Remount Section.	at
BARLIN	5.3.17		Division H.Q. moves to BARLIN and 36 M.V.S. to Mœuvres les MINES	at
	6.3.17		Visited units at HERSIN and 36 M.V.S.	at
	7.3.17		Visited 36 D.A.C. Houchin. 36 M.V.S. 194 Cys. A.S.C. + inspected H.Q. Horses went to joined from 2nd Bn's	at
	8.3.17		Visited HERSIN - M.M.P. Div Signals + no Section D.A.C.	at
	9.3.17		Visited 103, 104 Heav Coys. R.E. at SAINS-EN-GOHELLE. Monthly Conference Veterinary Officers + preparation of A.F. A2000.	at

2449 Wt. W14957/M90 750,000 1/16 J.B.C. & A. Forms/C.2118/12.

WAR DIARY
or
INTELLIGENCE SUMMARY

Army Form C. 2118.

Place	Date	Hour	Summary of Events and Information	Remarks and references to Appendices
BARLIN	10.3.17		Divisional D.A.C at HOUCHIN - 36th V. Section - 11th Divisional Train. Hourly interview with G.O.C Division.	
	11.3.17		36th V.S - 73rd Field Amb.lance.	
	12.3.17		Visits 36th V.S. and 106 Brigade R.F.A	
	13.3.17		Inspection with D.D.R. Field Army Surplus animals from 17: 72-73. Mobile Brigade + Machine Gun Companies. 45 animals on parade. 8. to M.B. for Veterinary Means - 16 pure ORs evacuated to Base Remount Army M.B. remainder to Field Remount Squadron.	
	14.3.17		36th V.S. - 33" Veteran Batt. Royal Fusiliers. VAUDRICOURT. BECHELM w. D.M.S.	
	15.3.17		Visits 36th V.S. & examined all animals (Remount Veterinary) for the Base approved for Signs of Stomatitis. a.b.	

WAR DIARY
or
INTELLIGENCE SUMMARY

Army Form C. 2118.

Place	Date	Hour	Summary of Events and Information	Remarks and references to Appendices
BARLIN	16.3.17		Weekly Conference. Officers preparation of A.F. A2009. Visits 104 Brigade R.F.A. at	
	17.3.17		Visited O.C. 3rd Canadian M.V.S. Kemmer from Stores Dept for the Divisional Artillery. Visits 36 Bde R.S. No 3. Section Reserve Park. All four member were heavy shellmen E.O. Division. Goed standard - have recommended at hellyshellmen to M.V.S.	
	18.3.17		Visited 36a V. Section. D.A.D.O.S regarding breakdown in Heddethat. Reports H.A.P. Staff that knift-me not sending in Compliance with instruction over inner by Division for compliance with instruction at	
	19.3.17		Visits 2n. D.A.C — 36 Bn V.S. 103. 104. 159 Field Companies. R.E. Complete arrangement for using Horse Dip with 3rd Canadian Division. at	
	20.3.17		Forward report on Horse To D.D.V.S. First Army — the Division to Inspection Mules affected Strace is about 1 Et 15. ay	

Army Form C. 2118.

WAR DIARY
or
INTELLIGENCE SUMMARY
(Erase heading not required.)

Place	Date	Hour	Summary of Events and Information	Remarks and references to Appendices
BARLIN	21.3.17		Initial 36 hr. v. S- visit at Pr SAINS + HERSIN. Divide half of B/106 Bde R.F.A. at	
	22.3.17		Visited No 3. Section of Reserve Park - Found two of exhibition to arrived - very little done to standing. Saw O.C. of Reserve Park informed him of the Condition of his animals and standings. at	
	23.3.17		Dipped half of B/105 Bde R.F.A. & arrived from O.D./106 Bde. at	
	24.3.17		Visited 36 MRS. & C/107 Bde R.F.A. T.O.K. Heavy Artillery cited with reference to O.K. Poor Chaff under at Barlin.	
	25.3.17		Attended with D.DVS. Inch-Army D.R. Recruits at Church Square. NOEUX LES MINES inspected place H.S. from Divisional Raids their animals here posted at once to Heavy Batteries R.G.A. at	

WAR DIARY or INTELLIGENCE SUMMARY

Army Form C. 2118.

Place	Date	Hour	Summary of Events and Information	Remarks and references to Appendices
BARLIN	26.3.17		Visited 36 H.S. and Noeux les Mines arranged for office at Bracquemont when Division leave Barlin. Signed report D/106 and same arrived from 2/c D.A.C. at	
	27.3.17		Visited 3 Divs. + inspected arrival of mountain 3 & Ed. of "Bainspark and 3 B.A.F.A.B D.A.C at Sains-en-Gohelle.	
	28.3.17		Visited 147 R.F.A.B (3 Batteries + Am. Column) at Verdrel Mont. Arrived in open + Several en billets. Same inspected in D.A.C	
	29.3.17		36 h.s. inspected arrival of mountain - Capt. J.J. O'Neill M.C. to the 147/R.F.A.B. see Cadet Office.	
	30.3.17		Visited A/14 A.F.A.Bde. held conference Veterinary Officers - Preparation of M.F. Moore - Capt. J. Bradley - V.O. % 14/R.F.A.B Cadet.	
	31.3.17		Visited 3 Can. Sect. D.A.C at Hesdigneul.	

CONFIDENTIAL.

Vol 20

WAR DIARY

of

A.D.V.S.

24th DIVISION.

From. 1-4-19.   To. 30-4-19.

VOL. 20.

WAR DIARY
INTELLIGENCE SUMMARY. ADVS. 24th Division

Army Form C. 2118.

(Erase heading not required.)

Hour, Date, Place	Summary of Events and Information	Remarks and references to Appendices

BARLIN 1-4-17	Conference of ADsVS at Headquarters 1st Army. Officer of DDVS. The following subjects were discussed:—
	1) Remounts or returning administration of Army. Corps or Divisions.
	2) Transport. Remounts by road to units at Front. Veterinary Personnel of Conducting Parties. — 1 Sergt Farrier or AVC Sergt attending Sick. Farriers Wallet.
	3) Veterinary Stores only to be obtained through usual channel.
	4) German attempt Tampered animals with B. Pullei.
	5) Equipment & personnel of Corps M.V. Section.
	6) Inspection for Conducting parties and receiving M.V.S. for relieving units of Sick during important operations:—
	  a) Corps M.V.S. from from Section in Corps
	  b) One Complete Foreman at without & Conducting parties from Base Title attached unit:—
	7) Remounts in charge upper Carted for by DVS. B.E.F.	

Army Form C. 2118.

WAR DIARY
or
INTELLIGENCE SUMMARY.
(Erase heading not required.)

Hour, Date, Place	Summary of Events and Information	Remarks and references to Appendices
Barlin. 1.4.17 (Sun.)	DVS. B.E.F. Clipping. a) Circumspection should be used opto Oct. & Nov, too [condition] due to exposure - underfeeding, and from time [supervision] aggravated by late clipping. b) However at any time for retention of skin disease. c) Disposal of horses dying on [m]arch or in line of march - responsibility rests with [unit]. d) Horse plants how a [Advance] supply. e) A.F. It 2000 for Army field artillery Bdes the nearest f) New I Division to which attached. g) Position of R.V.S's and Collecting posts to offensive [action]. Visits 36 th [section] and ADVS. 6th Div. Capt. J.H. ADAMS A.V.C. VO to 282 A.F.a.B.de asked to	
" 2-4-17	Visited VERDREL WOOD and inspected 147/A.F.a.Bde. Condition poor & amount of debilitated animals - 5 evacuated and 1 destroyed.	

WAR DIARY
INTELLIGENCE SUMMARY

Army Form C. 2118.

Hour, Date, Place	Summary of Events and Information	Remarks and references to Appendices
BARLIN. 2.4.17 (C.LD)	Nothing. A/14 A.F.A.Bde. 12 mounted and 13 dismounted. BAC/282 A.F.A.Bde. - 3 H.D. mounted.	
BRAQUEMONT. 3.4.17	24 Divin H.Q. Q&G moved to Sains-en-Gohelle. This Office moved to BRAQUEMONT. Inspected 34 L.D. animals & transport to field Remount Squadron - GONNEHEM. 3 L.D. Horses transferred to C/107 B.ac R.F.A. " 7 L.D. Horses & 20 Mules " " Field Remount Squadron. GONNEHEM. 2 L.D. Horses " " 36 MVS. 1 L.D. Horse slightly lame & unfit for immediate issue returned to Unit (74 Field Ambulance).	
" 4.4.17	Visited 104/ A.F.A.Bde and A/14 A.F.A.B at VERDREL WOOD. Visited 36 MVS. Inspected 14/H.A.B.A.C. encashed four cases of manure, 5 mules, 3 horses the others shipped. Visited D.H.Q. and C.R.A. inspection or condition of horses at VERDREL WOOD.	

WAR DIARY
INTELLIGENCE SUMMARY.
(Erase heading not required.)

Army Form C. 2118.

Hour, Date, Place	Summary of Events and Information	Remarks and references to Appendices
BRAQUEMONT 4-4-17 (Cont'd)	VERDREL WOOD — made following recommendation for 149/A.F.A. Bde and 14/A.F.A. Bde (less D.A.C.):— "Both retained to the end of the Battle for Button, for reasons of no worth."	
5.4.17	Inspected By C/10th Bde R.F.A. sent to Horse of Mines R.H.VS. Thirtable of B. and JC have disposed last week & arrangements have been made for further supplies. Tested 3 B.M.15, inspected animals to innoculate. Wire received from Division reporting No 6531 Sgt. ~~Pennell~~ Pennell, F.T.W. A.V.C. attached D/38 A.F.A. Bde. died of wounds. at ~~Pennell, F.T.W~~	
" 6.4.17	Weekly Conference Veterinary Officers. Properties of A.V.Dsns. Division & attached Units to be sent in separately. Capt. A. H. ADAMS A.V.C. No.? 262 A.F.A. Bde home on Retirement Charge to Capt. J.A.G. Gosling, A.V.C., left on " but for No.3. Veterinary Hospital, taking his two changes with him. Arrival & departure reported to A.D.V.S. First-Army.	

WAR DIARY
or
INTELLIGENCE SUMMARY

Army Form C. 2118.

Hour, Date, Place	Summary of Events and Information	Remarks and references to Appendices
BRAQUEMONT — 7.4.17	Visited A14/AF a Bde and BAC 147/AFaB. Held interview with OC Division and CRA. Visited No 2 Section of Reserve Park.	
8.4.17	196 Company ASC — Visited A.F.A Brigades at VERDREL WOOD. Met the three of 10/147 AFABs who had just opposition like Took same and went over her after. Talking with and to Wagon line Officers stating by. Sheds to evacuated & recommending the return of four horses be sent when going into NOEUX LES MINES. Pointed this to the Divisional artillery made some recommendation which was agreed with.	
9.4.17	Saw Staffs regarding horses busy stock-cropping help in their animal train. The boys hit to tops held the Polish Chapel. Visited 147 A. F.a.B informed DADVS that this lot Artillery was being necessary to time them. Visited D.A.D.Q.C.R.A. B/100 Bde R.F.A per troops three Bde ag at BETHUNE.	

WAR DIARY
or
INTELLIGENCE SUMMARY.
(Erase heading not required.)

Army Form C. 2118.

Hour, Date, Place	Summary of Events and Information	Remarks and references to Appendices
BRAQUEMONT. 10.4.17	Visits C/106 Bde R.F.A. - 36 M.V.S. and 10 Bdes at D.A.C. - This latter had lost horses at Snow Storm - 23 horses in 14th and 14 Army Field Arty Visits VERDREL WOOD and huts - My toes teeth - jelly Bde died from exposure in the night.	
" 11-4-17		
" 12.4.17	Visits VERDREL WOOD, horse standings. Anne & Shells 36 M.V.S. Have arrived Formation of Wrote to the village of VERDEIL. -	
" 13-4-17	Weekly Conference Veterinary Officers and Preparation of A.F. a 2000. Visits 1050. Saius and D/38, 68 and 88 Batteries 14 - Army Field Artillery Brigades. DDVS find horses F.a. fit for Sort & a litter. Spoke by wire :- 14 Army F. a. Bde - ADVS Fair - 68 Batty. Fair - 88 Battery Posi. - Ammunition Column Very good. 147 Army F. a. Bde H Battery Poor - 94 Batty Very Poor - 10 Batty. Fair - Ammunition Column Fair.	

WAR DIARY or INTELLIGENCE SUMMARY

Army Form C. 2118.

Hour, Date, Place	Summary of Events and Information	Remarks and references to Appendices
BRAQUEMONT 13-4-17	Fair. Also sent out a party to examine the condition of standings, exposed position of Mule lines, very bad, heavier being responsible for many losses. M.O.C.O. had made their present condition when he can has traced the heavy casualties much earlier. 14. A.F.A.B. had from A.D.S. from 4th Division. 6th R.F. Batteries from 4th Division — B.M.O. from 4 & 140 Divisions. forwarded to Staffs.	
" 14-4-17	Truck witnessed with A.A. Dn. L/c. deot grinder Divisional of Army, more reports on Army files Artillery Lives. No 85. S.277 P/4/Sgt Cawthorne E. A.V.C. arrived at D/38 A.F.A. Bde. in relief of No 6531 S.S. Pennell A.V.C.	
" 15-4-17	Cutting down office personnel to more in a forward direction.	
" 16-4-17	hooters arrivals P.D.H.Q. 282 A.F.A.B Am. Col. A/107. 147 A.F.A. Bde. v A/14 A.F.A.B. from 147 A.F.A.B 92 animals out R.M.V.S to severe debility.	

WAR DIARY
or
INTELLIGENCE SUMMARY.

(Erase heading not required.)

Army Form C. 2118.

Hour, Date, Place	Summary of Events and Information	Remarks and references to Appendices
BEAUMONT. 17.4.17	147 A.F.a.B moved to Aix Noulette. Conference 1st Division returning officers preparating for move.	
" 18.4.17	Visited D.H.Q. R.E. at SAINS-EN-GOHELLE.	
" 19.4.17	Inspected A.F.a 2000 (M.A.O.B.) & Impresa Opposite A.D.S's relieving divisions with all information re location of A.F.a.B.'s – M.V.S. Position – Test of Field Ambulances – Power chaff cutting machines of Division moved to NORRENT FONTES – 1st Artillery Brigade M.V. Section which remained to clear Artillery before move.	
NORRENT Fosse 20.4.17	Visited 1st Infantry Field Amb & D.D.M.S- First Army. Inspected A.F. a 2000 for Division Station billets for M.V.S. at FONTES.	
" 21. 4.17		
" 22-4-17	Visited 73 Infantry Brigade & 103 Field Company R.E.	

WAR DIARY
INTELLIGENCE SUMMARY.
(Erase heading not required.)

Army Form C. 2118.

Hour, Date, Place	Summary of Events and Information	Remarks and references to Appendices
NOREUIL FONTES. 23-4-17	Visited 72 Inf Bde. Part 1/17 Infantry Bde - and 191 Machine Gun Company.	
BONY 24-4-17	Division moved to BONY and MUST MATRINGHEM. The tone left behind 6 & 298 A.T. oB. at Bony. Australian Slaughter Cattle with Mallin - place put in of Guards, H.Qrs A.D.V.S. 1st Army, of	
" 25-4-17	Visited 36 M.V.S. 3 Rifle Brigade. 72 Field Ambulance and 9 East Surreys.	
" 26-4-17	1st and 73 Infantry Brigades moved to Baltune area and attached to 66 & 6th Divisions respectively. Visited 36 M.V.S. of	
" 27-4-17	Visited 39 M.V.S. Saw horses in march. heavy conference H.Qrs representation of A. a Sons. Inspected Iu D.A.C. 2 Section L.B. Echelon pour - No 1 Section Arrived. of	

Army Form C. 2118.

WAR DIARY
or
INTELLIGENCE SUMMARY.
(Erase heading not required.)

Hour, Date, Place	Summary of Events and Information	Remarks and references to Appendices
BOMY. 26.4.17	Visited 72 Infantry Bde. and 106 Bde R.F.A. A.B.D. Batteries fair. C Inspected. Found a number of superior skin sores in D Battery, notified same to B/Q.	
29.4.17	Visited 72 Infantry Bde. Group. Visited 107 Bde R.F.A. A/Som - B/ Inspected - C/fair. D/Orderly has moved to LIS Bouge. Visited 8/Queens West Surreys. Interviewed M.O. and Sergeant A.Y.C. A 106 Bde R.F.A at B.M.F. Section have unearthed a Skin Cases Tunnel. Have to be adopted into hut have [illegible] vigilance by the orderly by the examiner.	
30.4.17	Interviewed D.A.C. Division. R.A. H.Q. at A.D B.A.G. aj	

Confidential

Vol 21

War Diary

of

A.D.V.S.

24th Division.

From 1-5-17 To 31-5-17

Vol 21.

WAR DIARY
INTELLIGENCE SUMMARY. ADVS. 24th Division

Army Form C. 2118.

Hour, Date, Place	Summary of Events and Information	Remarks and references to Appendices
Bomy. 1-5-17	Visited D/107 Bde R.F.A. - 72 Field Ambulance - 103 Field Company R.E. regarding antibile grund. to C.C.S. 24 Div rate	
2-5-17	Visited 9/East Surreys - 1/North Staffords - 72 Machine Gun Company and 8/R. West Surreys. at	
3-5-17	Visited 108 Bde R.F.A. - 104 Field Company R.E. and saw I/o Remarks for Division of Renn's Rest Camp at THEROUANNE. L.B. diligent also Huts - 1st D. Band & repairs. Saw A.D.M.S. G.O.C. Division at	
4-5-17	Held Conference of M.O's in preparation of AFA2020. Winter 3 Evacuation at	
5-5-17	Interview G.O.C. Division 1.M.D.A.M.9. Visited 72 Infantry Brigade at	
6-5-17	Visited A.D.VS. whence reports have been sent note as Signed with Compliance bey. are not yet a supply of them - Conference of A.D.VS. 1st Army at Office of D.D.S. 1st Army	

WAR DIARY
INTELLIGENCE SUMMARY

Hour, Date, Place	Summary of Events and Information	Remarks and references to Appendices
Bony – 6 – S.77(Anx)	DDVS. 1st Army. at Army Head Quarters. Points discussed: — 1. Smoke Helmets for Horses. Allotment 1500 per Division. Instruction to meet Divisional Gas Officer. Same rec'd in consultation with Lieut Gas Officer. But a "Defensive measure" to be used for "Gas attack". MVS to make issue that Army M V Section Reprints Ann Helmets to be sent to S.H.R. Depôt Abbeville. 2. Contagious Ophthalmia. 3. Rest Camps Remounts losing condition. 4. Shells The Strainer by Sergt A.V.C. 5. Dipping Animals on Strength of Some April: A line. 6. Australian Expn. Force in Tin. Chick would harbour as activity to the amputate of same.	

WAR DIARY
or
INTELLIGENCE SUMMARY.

Army Form C. 2118.

Hour, Date, Place	Summary of Events and Information	Remarks and references to Appendices
Bomy. 6-5-17 (Sun)	Visited Section of 191 Machine Gun Company at La Pierre - Robecq - Lapugnoy - Nr Aire. at	
" 7-5-17	Same. Visited 24 D.M.C and 194 Company A.S.C and 36 M.T. Section at	
" 8-5-17	Visited Flaming huts with C.R.E. Division 103 and 104 Field Companies R.E. also, A+B/106 Bde R.F.A and B/107 Bde R.F.A. at Lyi. Bomy.	
" 9-5-17 Norrent Fontes.	Annie Norrent Fontes. 36th Section March Fontes.	
" 10-5-17	P/A/Serjt No9262 Litherland.T. A.V.C reduced from R.P. Private for insubordination to S.M.T by O.C. B/106 Bde R.F.A. at	
" 11-5-17	Weekly conference of Veterinary Officers and inspection of W.F. at 10 am. Interview with 9.0.C. Division who is leaving on 12th for Another Command. at Norrent Fontes.	
Drogland. 12-5-17	Leave Norrent Fontes - Arrive Drogland. at	

WAR DIARY or INTELLIGENCE SUMMARY

Army Form C. 2118.

Hour, Date, Place	Summary of Events and Information	Remarks and references to Appendices
DROGLANDT. 13-5-17	Visited hunts of 17 & 72 Infantry Brigade in STEENVOORDE AREA. also 183, 104 & 39 Field Cey. R.E. &	
" 14-5-17	Visited R.A.H.Q. and 34 D.M.S. hoes Capt. J. Blackburn. M.C. to 107 Bde R.F.A. which had proceeding to Ypres Salient. DDVS. Second Army orders. &	
" 15-5-17	Rem DROGLANDT.	
BRANDHOEK 16-5-17	Anne BRANDHOEK. Rem Poperinghe AREA. & Visited 36 Ch. V. Section and ADSVS 41st and 55th Divisions Inspected three Dips and Anti-gas Respirators with the latter. &	
" 17-5-17	Visited 106 Bde R.F.A. and AVC and 194 C. Asst. i/c CASSEL AREA. Reported Veterinary Equipment of C. i/c M.B. 106 Bde R.F.A. Powell AVC Wote 106 Bde R.F.A. Visited Horse R. at St JANS CAPPEL in arrange for the arrival of the Friends on 18-5-17. &	

WAR DIARY
INTELLIGENCE SUMMARY

Army Form C. 2118.

Hour, Date, Place	Summary of Events and Information	Remarks and references to Appendices
BRANDHOEK. 18-5-17	Weekly Conference Veterinary Officers preparation of A.T. Accns. prior discussed. Horse Rope- And gas respirators Mk.II noted – Skinning Yard arrived. Visits 36 Inf Section. In field Veterinary equipment of Cpl. N.A. Macgregor Atl. 19th Bn. Brit. train. Capt. ROGERS Mil. 30ths arrived as clerk during absence of Pte. TRAYETT – A.S.E. who proceeds on special leave home this month. Grants 4th Army at Arrival of 34th Divisional Signal Company Troops Kemp to Adj. of St Jans Cappel off.	
19-5-17	Pte. h. TRAYETT Clerk to ADVS went on leave to England from 19.5.17 – 18-6-17 (First Army 943/360 A. Returned to Army had him out at PoPerINGHE 103-104. 12 griess Crys R.S. 5 horse Squ "H.M.P. Visits 36 In Sand Og/R Sussex Regt C. Col.	

Army Form C. 2118.

WAR DIARY
~~INTELLIGENCE SUMMARY~~
(Erase heading not required.)

Instructions regarding War Diaries and Intelligence Summaries are contained in F. S. Regs., Part II. and the Staff Manual respectively. Title pages will be prepared in manuscript.

Hour, Date, Place	Summary of Events and Information	Remarks and references to Appendices
BRANDHOEK. 19.5.17 (cont'd)	Summary:-	
" 20.5.17	Anti-gas Hose respirators to New pattern demonstration with Anti-gas respirators helmets at 36th R. with Divisional Gas Officer. The following points noted which were discussed with Respirator:- 1. Elastic too short. 2. Keep hose from misuse. 3. Bottom not securely sewn in. This took hour wearing his box helmet to adjust a new Respirator. Visited A.D.S. & 4th Division reinforcement Atma Respirator for three Respirators demonstration at 3 Lieuts 6 7 & 73 Infantry Brigades Machine Gun Company. 72.73. 74 Field Ambulances - One Officer one N.C.O.	
" 21.5.17	attender from each. Visited VIII Corps Horse Depot at Poperinghe- 72 & Brigade Machine Gun Company practising dispersal.	

WAR DIARY

INTELLIGENCE SUMMARY

Army Form C. 2118.

Hour, Date, Place	Summary of Events and Information	Remarks and references to Appendices
BRANDHOEK. 22-5-17	Stretcher Bearers's demonstration at 36 hrs.15 to:— 72 Inf. Bde. Machine Gun Company, 10th Train Company R.E. Employment and Tree Company of 24 Div— Train.	
	Visits VIII Corps Stretcher Bearer Sch.f — 17th Infantry Brigade — Machine Gun Company and Stretcher Bearers of Stretcher Bearers demonstration at 36 hrs.S to:— H.Q. R.A. 107 Bde R.F.A. - Rifle Brigade - 103 + 129 Field Companies R.E.	
	Visits Boesinghe Ps Gene demonstration on Stretcher bearers to 7th Div. Signal Company 73 Infantry Brigade and Machine Gun Company from Temp VIIIth Corps Stretcher Bearer Sch.	
23-5-17	S.E. No. 16983 Sejt:— MARTIN. H.O. MK. arrived for duty with B/105 Bde R.F.A.	

Army Form C. 2118.

WAR DIARY
or
INTELLIGENCE SUMMARY.
(Erase heading not required.)

Instructions regarding War Diaries and Intelligence Summaries are contained in F. S. Regs., Part II. and the Staff Manual respectively. Title pages will be prepared in manuscript.

Hour, Date, Place	Summary of Events and Information	Remarks and references to Appendices
BRANDHOEK 24.5.17	Gas demobilised to 2nd D.A.C. at Ryveldt, and 194 Company at Cassel	
25.5.17	2E No 9262 Pte LITHERLAND. T., A.V.C. from B/106 Bde R.F.A. proceeded to No 2 Veterinary Hospital - Havre. at	
	Health Conference Melhuish, officer in preparation PAF.H.2000. Proceed with O.C. 36 bn.F.Section. B/Queen River Sneyd and 24 D.A.C. of	
26.5.17	visits 36 bn. F. Section.	
27.5.17	visits A.D.V.S. 41st Division regarding evacuation from Army	
	Area A Ashley Brig-in. at	
28.5.17	36 h. V.S. hurried to C.32 Co. 1	(Sheet 28).
	30 Divn M.B. occupied the Villa near Poperinghe. at	
29.5.17	Visited Remount Stage Camp near HAZEBROUCK. Saw 203	
	Remits HD. good. I.D. Mules some good. Attention overspan at	
	with officers Mins - Hurlegoed - R. Poot. at	
30.5.17	Lft. BRANDHOEK.	
RENINGHELST.	Arrive RENINGHELST at	

WAR DIARY
or
INTELLIGENCE SUMMARY
(Erase heading not required.)

Army Form C. 2118.

Hour, Date, Place	Summary of Events and Information	Remarks and references to Appendices
RENINGHELST. 31-5-17	Visited H.Q. Camp 24 D.M.C. & issue of Remounts. Took over all remount Hand Chargers & despatched team to 36 M.S. Section. (There were at Reninghem Hand Chargers remounts for remounts of unit). Visited 8/Buffs. 73 - 74 Field Ambulances. 9/Northumb. 9/ Remounts. Visited 36 M.I.S & discussed job of unit. Dept. - Saw ADVS 41st Div. said Section Comd. wd deal with any pure sick at present. ADVS 41st Division himself was a Veterinary Walet. Visited 191 Machine Gun Company. Gave Gas demonstration to 191 Machine Gun Company. a.k.	

CONFIDENTIAL.

War Diary

of

D.A.D.V.S

24th Division.

From 1-6-17. To 30·6·17.

Vol. 22.

WAR DIARY
INTELLIGENCE SUMMARY. ADVS. 24TH DIVISION

Army Form C. 2118.

(Erase heading not required.)

Hour, Date, Place	Summary of Events and Information	Remarks and References to Appendices
RENINGHELST. 1-6-17	Held Conference of Veterinary Officers re preparation of A.F. A.Z.00.	
2-6-17	Visited 36th V. Section ob.	
3-6-17	Visited 36th V. Section and 19, 72 Infantry Brigades ob. Visited Hd.qrs branch Sanitary D.D.V.S. Second Army. DDR. Visited 196 & 197 Company A.S.C. RENINGHELST stables ob.	
4-6-17	Visited 3 Sqdns. 36th V. Section. RENINGHELST Stables. Checked the new office & the hut dressings. ob.	
5-6-17	Visited 7 Infantry Brigade. 191 Machine Gun Coy. Visited 3 Stables & remained with following operators. Gave instruction for Advanced Collecting & Dressing Post & returned to B-Visit ob.	
6-6-17	Advanced Check Post of 36 h.VS. moved to G.3.r.b.3.c (Sht/28) Visited 24 D.M.C. ob.	
7-6-17	Visited 36 h.VS, Inf Bde - D.M.C. Offensive Commenced at WYTSCHAETE - MESSINES S. ob.	

WAR DIARY
INTELLIGENCE SUMMARY
(Erase heading not required.)

Army Form C. 2118.

Hour, Date, Place	Summary of Events and Information	Remarks and References to Appendices
RENINGHELST. 8-6-17	Weekly Conference of Veterinary Officers. Preparation of A.F. A 2002. Reputation Chevron Officers Chief Medals of Cpls T. BLACKBURN A.V.C. and J.K. HARRIS A.V.C. for certain deficiencies which were reported. Capt I.R. BARNES M/C Chief did not compete. Mules 106 Bde R.F.A. Sub-Dist Horse of Battalion all doing well.	
9-6-17	Visited 106 and 107 Bde R.F.A. Sub-Dist Horses of C/107 - 25% hall. 2 rather severe. Animals evacuated to Division during preparation. "Morning Carrying up of ration & ammunition thru' YPRES & YLIENT & Town - Ridden 4.4. hours of Shell fire SS. Success practically whole of C/106 Bde R.F.A. and 25% Horses of C/107 Bde R.F.A. regarding gassed animals they were suddenly caught in	

WAR DIARY
or
INTELLIGENCE SUMMARY.
(Erase heading not required.)

Army Form C. 2118.

Hour, Date, Place	Summary of Events and Information	Remarks and References to Appendices
RENINGHELST 9-6-17	Caught in enfilade shell burrage. One team stopped. Field vet. hire animals got medic. lot a still hit wagon. Pleated at his throat. The remainder galloped at Manger Zone. Always treat these for tetanus & the animals & Du DAVS meanwhile. No 1. Sect 2n DAVS moved through Dip at POPERINGHE say RRR - Second Army regarding exchange of S.I.C. 72 Infantry Brigade. Visited 36 units and 73 Inf. Bde.	
10.6.17		
11.6.17	Visited 72 Inf Bde - 36 Units.	
12.6.17	DDVS. Second Army about exhaustion - Report about peonies' animals - Sick Horse to OC. 7th Pl Advanced.	
13.6.17	D.H.Q. left RENINGHELST Arrived H31 b 5·2 nr Onderdom (Sheet 28)	
H31 b 5·2 14.6.17	Visited 2n DMS - 17·72·73 Inf. Bdes. 36 units home to NICURTIN (Sheet 28).	(Sheet 28)

WAR DIARY
or
INTELLIGENCE SUMMARY.
(Erase heading not required.)

Army Form C. 2118.

Hour, Date, Place	Summary of Events and Information	Remarks and References to Appendices
H3/65:2(28) 14.6.17 (Cont'd)	36 hours hard to N.1 Section (Shed 28) The following attached to Veterinary Administration :- 23rd Divisional Artillery D.A.C. Nos 189, 298, 315 Bde. Army Field Artillery. 4 Mobile Vet Sec – On Instruction. Beth – on Cavalerie Travelling Companies. On Canadian Railway troops of Health Conference Veterinary Officers preparation M.P. Army Trials 191 R.G. Coy and 315 Pate C.F.C.I.T. Sgt. Shepherd A.V.C. attached 73rd F.Bde reduced to Corporal for being Compulsory to until Corporal for non-compliance with an order. Promise in writing when Pte Humphrey T.Mo2 Vet. Hospital, Havre. (refer O/C AVC Base Records and applied for a relief. before his veterinary experience from Catalin deficiency.	
15.6.17		

Form/C. 2118/11.

WAR DIARY
INTELLIGENCE SUMMARY
(Erase heading not required.)

Army Form C. 2118.

Hour, Date, Place	Summary of Events and Information	Remarks and References to Appendices
H31b5.2 (Rw/28) 16.6.17	Found instructions for A Divisional Veterinary Officer to report 1st day of each month. deficiencies to Officer Cmdg Veterinary returnees. Wants Orderlies when this returnees change. An explanation to account for deficiencies. Railhead Point at Ordeardon Siding H30b central (8w/28) Shelters. 8 H.R. Rifles. 24.D. How. & Brigade at F.A. Rifles. Remnd one Officer when shell arrived 1 Capt. to Ambulance to 36 hrs. Violets 36 hrs. S. 194 and 196 boys A.S.C. at	
17.6.17	Violets No 2 Section DAC at No2 Bde R.7.a and 36 hrs. of	
18.6.17	315 Army Bde R.F.A. left Hopetrees 298 Army Bde R.F.A. ab arriving in Good Condition. 103 Bde R. Fd 23 Division Ardillin Fair. S/Queen Trainport. at	

WAR DIARY
or
INTELLIGENCE SUMMARY.
(Erase heading not required.)

Army Form C. 2118.

Hour, Date, Place	Summary of Events and Information	Remarks and References to Appendices
H31 b 5.2 (Sheet 29) 19-6-17	Visit Service Squadron of VI Inns Killing Dragoons. Saw 24 Horses for 24 Divisional Kitchen. 3 b.w.s. od	
20.6.17	Attended Conference under Director of Veterinary Services at S. OMER. Subject "Administrative duties of Corps ADsVS. Visit Remount Halt near HAZEBROUCK & examined 132 Remounts for this Division. K.R Horses. Mules good - Risen my id/Nuent. ag	
21.6.17	Inspected 189 Army Bde. R.F.A A/34 Batt. Poor. B/ fair. C/ Good. D/ fairly good. BMC good. Sent to 8 Horse to 3 Shell Bom Bardier @ Deklitz. Injur 3 Dwept Arms Army sick Animals 72. 10-12 f. Wet are Ambulance Cases - 5 Find Horses (3R.2LDs) Lt Freane Whyties handed Work to DDVS. Seen Army. Visits Jaunport of 3 Rifle Brigade.	

Forms/C. 2118/11.

WAR DIARY
or
INTELLIGENCE SUMMARY.
(Erase heading not required.)

Army Form C. 2118.

Hour, Date, Place	Summary of Events and Information	Remarks and References to Appendices
H31/6.5.2 (Shed/28)		
21-6-17 (Cont'd)	No S.E. 18479/S.4 Pt TRAVETT, M. A.S.C. Clerk to A.D.V.S returned from leave.	
22.6.17	Health Conference of Veterinary Officers forwarded A.F.a.2000. Visits 17 & 73 Infantry Bdes. of 106 Bde R.F.A.	
23.6.17	Visits 36th V Sectn. of 106 Bde R.F.A. Mule TX DNIS. 2 Army re evacuation to Base are 92 Cases awaiting evacuation at 36th V Sectn. of 106 Bde R.F.A.	
24-6-17	Visits 36th V Sectn. 100-130th R.F.A.	
25.6.17	Visits 107 Bde R.F.A. and 19 Infantry Bde. at	
26.6.17	Visits of DDC - 179, Machine Gun Company, at	
27.6.17	Visits No 26 a.f.a.s.De. - A Batt Mule Goat Horses from Some regt from Bronvie / Mense.	
	117/Batty- Gondulin train - Spencer 2 beeren Coul.	
	117/Batty- Gondulin Fault, foot.	
	26/Bac Coot. at	

Army Form C. 2118.

WAR DIARY
or
INTELLIGENCE SUMMARY.
(Erase heading not required.)

Instructions regarding War Diaries and Intelligence Summaries are contained in F. S. Regs., Part II. and the Staff Manual respectively. Title pages will be prepared in manuscript.

Hour, Date, Place	Summary of Events and Information	Remarks and References to Appendices
H31 b5.2 (Sheet 28) 28.6.17	Preparing France to new area. Training and Divisional train.	
CAESTRE 29.6.17	Hune to Caestre.	
LUMBRES 30.6.17	Armies IX M.B.R.E.S. En route at a new dispatches to M.M.R. 2nd Army.	

CONFIDENTIAL.

War Diary.

of

D.A.D.V.S.

24th Division

From 1-7-17. To 31-7-17.

Vol. 23.

WAR DIARY
or
INTELLIGENCE SUMMARY.   ADMS - 24 DIVISION

Army Form C. 2118.

Hour, Date, Place	Summary of Events and Information	Remarks and References to Appendices

LUMBRES. 1-7-17   Weekly interview with D.M.S. Division. Visited ADMS. Second Army regarding transferring of Captain J. Blackburn. Arr. V.O. & 107 Bde R.F.A. to another Division. X Corps. ADMS & to inform Army regarding transfer - have received letter by 2nd Division "A" G.M.C. Division directs that this officer is not to proceed until Division receives orders from X Corps A.

2-7-17   Interviewed ADVS X Corps. Visited 6/ Queens transport at ?.

3-7-17   Visited 72 + 73 Infantry Brigades ob- to machine gun ADMS X Corps. Visited Blaringhem (hygiene-25" Imp.) Inspected 11 Wing Riding Depôt Bollezeele, R.F.C. regarding the case of Aeroplane Mechanic at improving sept. Fm. 2nd Stowe N2 Medics with my slight skin affection. All her his water and army for him ? Lieut. Leap. H.C. deemed a very competent M.O.

WAR DIARY
or
INTELLIGENCE SUMMARY.
(Erase heading not required.)

Army Form C. 2118.

Hour, Date, Place	Summary of Events and Information	Remarks and References to Appendices

LUMBRES. 3-7-17 (Cont'd.)

Corporal N.C.O. trades 1 Coy. R.E. and 104 Field Company R.E. at same place.

4-7-17 — Proceeded on leave to Rhyl. Capt. N. A. MacGREGOR R.A.M.C. appointed to take during my absence from 4-14 inst. The following events to have occurred during my absence:—

Notification received from Staff Capt. 2nd Divisional Artillery that Capt. T. Blackburn R.A.M.C. left 2nd D.A.C. for duty with "C" Casualty Division on 3rd inst. A/DMS 2nd Army. A.D.M.S. Corps & 2nd Division H.Q. notified.

5-7-17 — Notification from Staff Captain 2nd Divisional Artillery that 2 Lts. now proceed to Rest Camp.

Capt. N.A. MacGregor and Inspector 38 Reserve it. Found one case suspicious. Change used to 3 6h.h.S. Notice read to all ranks. Football inspected daily, all remain in P.U.O. days. Forwarded recommendation for Sergt. Appleby 36 bath the for his k. P/A/Staff Sergeant to O.R. AVC Clerk, there at

WAR DIARY
INTELLIGENCE SUMMARY.
(Erase heading not required.)

Army Form C. 2118.

Hour, Date, Place	Summary of Events and Information	Remarks and references to Appendices
LUMBRES. 6-7-17	A.F.A 2118 prepared & copy sent to ADVS. 2nd Corps. ADVS. 2nd Army wires "Daily wire not required at present". O.C. 36 M.V.S. notified.	
	36 M.V.S. arrived LaBelle Croix - replaces Mobilis. & ADVS IX Corps. in 2nd Division. Q.	(attached as 5th Regt)
	As to return received from 1/1 West Riding Heavy Battery R.G.A. Capt. MacGREGOR AV. proceeded to Ebblinghem & found him had left the area. Capt. Torvell AV. who had been detailed as D.O. informed of the departure. 106 & 107 Bdes R.F.A. - 194 Company A.S.C. and 36 M.V.S. rejoined Division in Rest Area.	
7.7.17	Capt. MacGREGOR AV. advised about IV ADVS IX Corps. to recommend a Veterinary Officer to command the M.V.S.	
8.7.17	194 Machine Gun Company rejoined Division from 2nd Army HQ. Capt. MacGregor AV. took over veterinary charge of	

WAR DIARY
or
INTELLIGENCE SUMMARY.

(Erase heading not required.)

Army Form C. 2118.

Hour, Date, Place	Summary of Events and Information	Remarks and references to Appendices
LUMBRES. 9-7-17	Applied to ADVS. 2nd Corps Farriage Veterinary attendance for the Field Company R.E., 12 "Skinner Traction" and 1/Section 2nd DAC by	
10-7-17	Warning Order received regarding move of Division. Applied to ADVS. 8 Corps Farriage Veterinary attendance for 129 Field Company R.E. Capt M.A. MacGREGOR AVC visited 36th I/S regarding move of	
11-7-17	Notification from 'Q' that 148 Remount to be at Divisional Artillery Hd. arriving on 13" inst. Arranged with Capt. S.H. LAWRIE AVC to inspect same on arrival at	
12-7-17	Received instructions from ADVS 2nd Corps regarding a Conference on 14" inst. at	
13-7-17	A.F. A2010 forwarded recently to ADVS 2 Corps. Operation Orders received from C.R.A. regarding move of Artillery and 3 bh.A.S. commencing on 13" inst. at	
14-7-17	Capt MACGREGOR AVC inspected arrival of remounts to S" OMER.	

WAR DIARY
or
INTELLIGENCE SUMMARY.

Army Form C. 2118.

(Erase heading not required.)

Hour, Date, Place	Summary of Events and Information	Remarks and references to Appendices
LUMBRES. 14.7.17	Execution to St OMER.	
	Copy of letter from II Army received from 2nd Division "Q" regarding returning arrangements for wounded officers' horses and animals. Capt Munro proceeded to 3 F.A.V.S. Wounded Animals. Capy Munro proceeded to 3 F.A.V.S.	
	D.A.D.V.S. returned from leave. Applies arrived to A.D.V.S. 2nd Corps and 2nd Division "Q" by	
15.7.17	Inspected 73 F.B. and 191 Machine Gun Company. - Dealt with correspondence that had arrived during my absence. etc	
16.7.17	Reported personally to A.D.V.S. 2nd Corps at Hoop-Oust, at	(Sheet 28)
17.7.17	Visited 19 Infantry Brigade. - hq Chief P. TRAVETT. Also applies sick sent to C.C.S. of TRAVETT. Also applies sick sent to C.C.S. of 3/Rifle Brigade. Was walking to the river	
18.7.17	Arthurs a rider of 3/Rifle Brigade. Was walking to the river when h collided with a broken bottle + completely severed left hind. Horse destroyed - Turned all sick returns to 2nd Division Q. APM. Arranged with O.C. 23 Veterinary Hospital Licques for animals left behind Licques to	

Army Form C. 2118.

WAR DIARY
or
INTELLIGENCE SUMMARY.
(Erase heading not required.)

Instructions regarding War Diaries and Intelligence Summaries are contained in F.S. Regs., Part II. and the Staff Manual respectively. Title pages will be prepared in manuscript.

Hour, Date, Place		Summary of Events and Information	Remarks and references to Appendices
LUMBRES.	19.7.17	Left Lumbres.	
STEENVOORDE	"	Arrived STEENVOORDE.	
		Capt. ROGERS. A.V.C. 36th Bde arrived to act as temporary Clerk during the absence of Pte TRIVETT sick.	
	20.7.17	Held a conference of Veterinary Officers and Preparation of P.F. A2000.	
	21.7.17	Conference of DAD'sVS at II Corps Head quarters. Visited 12/R: Fusiliers.	
"	22.7.17	Visited 14th Infantry Brigade.	
"	23.7.17	Left STEENVOORDE.	
ZEVECOTEN	23.7.17	Arrived ZEVECOTEN — Handed over the attached 8th Division to DDVS 8th/IIIs.	
		23rd Division.	
	5 p.m.	Sent in 16/74 Field Ambulance — RENINGHELST on account of 2nd Lieut Turtle Meier, at Capt. H.A. MACGREGOR A.V.C. answering fire.	

Army Form C. 2118.

WAR DIARY
or
INTELLIGENCE SUMMARY.
(Erase heading not required.)

Instructions regarding War Diaries and Intelligence Summaries are contained in F. S. Regs., Part II. and the Staff Manual respectively. Title pages will be prepared in manuscript.

Hour, Date, Place	Summary of Events and Information	Remarks and references to Appendices
ZEVECOTEN. 24-7-17	In Field Ambulance, ch	
" 25-7-17	Returned to state of	
	Visited Veterinary Officers of the Division	
	Capt- J.A. LAURIE, M.B. POWELL M.A. MACGREGOR	
	Visits 36 b.A.S. of MVS receive Advance Part N266.9. Shul 28.	
" 26-7-17	Visits 36 b.V. Section and 106 Bde R.F.A. at	
" 27-7-17	Weekly Conference of Veterinary Officers - preparation	
	of Palemo.	
	Examined 10 three precaution c/36 A.V.S.	
P.M.	Enemy Aircraft dropped bombs in vicinity. Heavy casualties	
	amongst animals in neighbouring Division.	
	Visits 86 army Brie Artillery Brigade A B C D and	
	B.A.C. at	
" 28-7-17	Visits 36 blent and 1.2.3 Section 24 D.A.C.	
	Visits Nos 1.2.3.4 Companies Col 24 Divisional Train	
	with 2nd Corps Headquarters and ADVS.	

WAR DIARY
or
INTELLIGENCE SUMMARY

(Erase heading not required.)

Army Form C. 2118.

Place	Date	Hour	Summary of Events and Information	Remarks and references to Appendices
ZEVECOTEN	28.7.17 (Cont'd)		and A.D.S. Hourly relieving H.A.A.G. Division.	
"	29.7.17		Visits 36th. V. Section.	
"	30.7.17		Visits 107 Bde. R.F.A. – 191 Machine Gun Company. 12/Royal Fusiliers. Visits 36th. V. Section, examined 3 Frenchmen for evacuation by Rail. Visits 52/Army Field Artillery Brigade.	
"	31.7.17		Visits 36th. V. Section. Visits 298/Army Field Artillery Bde. Sent to one Frenchman - O.Batg. 2, B.Batg. - 1. Inspection 117 Remounts for Division.	

CONFIDENTIAL.

WAR DIARY

of

D.A.D.V.S

24th DIVISION.

From 1-8-14   To 31-8-14.

VOL. 24.

Army Form C. 2118.

WAR DIARY
or
INTELLIGENCE SUMMARY

(Erase heading not required.)

DADVS. 24th DIVISION

Place	Date	Hour	Summary of Events and Information	Remarks and references to Appendices
ZEVECOTEN	1-8-17		Visited 3 Btn. V. Section and examined 20 cases of evacuation by train. Capt. D.R. Bartley O/C. Prepared a draft Official Buck. Inspection his Diary to whole Officer Bull. Des. recd. Central Expos. to Oth. Records - est. Mentioned. 94	
"	2-8-17		Visited 3 Btn. V. Section - No. 1 Section 23rd D.T.C. + 190 Company ASC from Opl.Talmort Corner - 14 Machine Gun Company. Cpl. Howard and 52/ A.F. A. 1311 order. ADVS. 2nd Corps asked regarding evacuation of Sick Horse Cases to be sent to II Corps Mobile Veterinary Detachment. R.F.C. — Hope this very muddy affair which animals waded up. Visited D/106 Bde. at /animals crossed. /	
"	3-8-17		Weekly Conference of Veterinary Officers - Preparation of A.F. A.5000. 94	
"	4-8-17		Conference of DADVS's at ADVS. Office - 2nd Corps. Weekly Wilson Conference :— Reduction of horses affecting A.V.C personnel - Opl.Talmie - Entraining/evacuation/ prior arrival from 2nd Corps M.V. Det 45. Compilation of Evacuation R.Rets. - Certificate rendered in reverse "Cynal Diaries" "Certified that all cases mentioned have been proceeded to Base to full extent treatment that they are free from Contagious Diseases including Stomatitis."	

WAR DIARY or INTELLIGENCE SUMMARY

Place	Date	Hour	Summary of Events and Information	Remarks and references to Appendices
ZEVECOTEN	4-8-17 (Cont'd)		Stomatitis. Schick: now Plt. map Missing animals. Animal found. Delay in returning Receipt Vouchers to Base Petty Stores — Veterinary Equipment — Divisional Burial Officer to bury dead animals — Disposal of same — Seeding in a number of Substitutes of R.V. Section. Examined 23 animals at 3 Ch. V. Section. Remonstration. off	
"	5-8-17		Visited 2" Corps M.V. Det'mt with 58 animals for evacuation. Visited 73" Field Ambulance. off	
"	6-8-17		Visited 36h. V. Section. km 6 of 72" Infantry Brigade. off	
"	7-8-17		Accompanied DDVS V Army & ADVS 2" Corps who inspected 108 Brigade R.F.A. DDVS remarks on condition of Off'rs Batt'y R.A. Canvas, Shoe brain of animals. Examination of Sick. Instructed C.O. 5 Brigade for Brigade - Sick. horse - Impact. Watering arrangements. Also visited 3 Ch. V. Section. DDVS expressed satisfaction with arrangements at Section.	
"	p.m.		Visited 3 Ch. V. S. Examined 36 animals for evacuation by road. off	

Army Form C. 2118.

WAR DIARY
or
INTELLIGENCE SUMMARY
(Erase heading not required.)

Instructions regarding War Diaries and Intelligence Summaries are contained in F. S. Regs., Part II. and the Staff Manual respectively. Title Pages will be prepared in manuscript.

Place	Date	Hour	Summary of Events and Information	Remarks and references to Appendices
ZEVECOTEN	8.8.17		Visited 36th M.V. Section, D Batty 702 Bde R.F.A., D Batty 29th Army F.A. Bde. and B.A.C. 86 Army F.A. Bde. A te Fr. Battery there are a number of suspected Mange Cases ex isolated. Gave instruction F.V.O. % to examine & scrapings at 36 M.V.S. at	
"	9.8.17		Visited 36 M.V.S., examined horses for mange by steam. Also scrapings from suspected Mange cases J.B.A.C. /86 F.A. Bde. A.R.C. 36 M.V.S. myself visited to demonstrate. Arranged schedule F.V.O. % to take morning scrapings daily until further orders. Visited 17 F.A. Bde. at	
"	10.8.17		Weekly Conference of Veterinary Officers. Preparation of A.F. A.2033 at	
"	11.8.17		Parades inspection on transport lines in early morning – 1 R. Rifles. 1 London, 1 H.D. Yeomanry. A.D.M.S. Signal Company. Inspected 86/Army F.A. Bde., 1st & 12th Royal Fusiliers, 93rd Field Ambulance. Weekly interview held by O.C. Mobile sections A.D/ 106 Bde R.F.A. sick & animals of Division. at	

WAR DIARY
INTELLIGENCE SUMMARY

Place	Date	Hour	Summary of Events and Information	Remarks and references to Appendices
ZEVECOTEN	12.8.17		Conference of A.D's V.S at 2nd Corps H.Q. Subjects:- Daily Casualty State - Stationary Office & M.V.S army OR. dry feed R.L.S. - Complaints from Sick Horse Units of Evacuating parties refusing to accept N.C.O's & animals sent to Corps M.V.D but which have developed heat - lice - epizootic Lymphangitis. Same army 6 small personnel Clipping - Shoy Front and Animals - Horse Bty - Preservation of Pas by M.V.S. Ariel mat Temp. Emp. M.V. Dept. Visited 8 Ca.V. Section - examined 42 road cases. Visited Rod Section - 24 S.A.V.C. examined recruits, armies Remounts - Mules, army front - Horse green. One H.D. led echu regimen. at	
"	13.8.17		Visited D/106 Bde R.F.A. C/104 Bde R.F.A. 36 units examined 25 cases. A incurvation by train. Visited 2nd Corps. M.V. Sect. regarding Train Cases. at	
"	14.8.17		Visited 3 units. 2nd Corps M.V. Section resumed entraining Train cases. at	

WAR DIARY or INTELLIGENCE SUMMARY

Army Form C. 2118.

Place	Date	Hour	Summary of Events and Information	Remarks and references to Appendices
ZEVECOTEN	15.8.17		Visited 11/King's Liverpool Rg^t (Pioneers), 13/Sherwood Foresters (Pioneers) - 72nd Field Ambulance - and 36 N.V. Section. at	
"	16.8.17		Visited 36th W.Section, examined 39 cases of evacuation. Took over of Stirrup attachments in a hunting case from B/46Bde R.F.A. 14th Division. Inspected A.D.V.S - 2nd Corps 170 % sick - horses T.R. animals, surplus charges for transfer. at	
"	17.8.17		Weekly Conference Veterinary Officers. Her^d of Army Field Artillery Bde reports circul^d to A.D.V.S Corps with their A.F.A. Bdes. Visited D.A.C Bath, A/10thBde R.F.A. Saw O.C. Division regarding Ophthalmia. at	
"	18.8.17		Visited D.A.Bath 7/7 Bde R.F.A. The O.C D.Bath gave me his animals sick. The grooms while feeding reported b/ O.C Division / C.A. Captⁿ J.R BARKER. are returned from leave. Visited 36th V.S examined 54 animals for horse transfer. Returned G.O.C Division and A.D.V.S.	ack.

WAR DIARY
or
INTELLIGENCE SUMMARY

(Erase heading not required.)

Army Form C. 2118.

Place	Date	Hour	Summary of Events and Information	Remarks and references to Appendices
ZEVECOTEN	19.8.17		Visited ADVS. 2 Corps re evacuation & retirement Officers' horses. Visited 36 M.V.S.	
"	20.8.17		Visited 10.6 and 107 Bde R.F.A. D/52 Army FA Bde. 19, H.Q. Coy. 36 M.V.S. Bombs dropped on horse lines in early hours morning of	
	21.8.17		Visited 17th and 73rd Infantry Bdes – also Water Supply to animals at Micmac Camp with MO & Sanitary Officers. Visited 2nd Corps M.V. Det. 36 M.V.S and 5th animal for evacuation.	
	22.8.17		Visited 2nd DTMS – 36 MVS. 5 Horses Killed – 12 Wounded at 1st Field Sqdn RE by shell fire in horse lines during early hours of morning. of	
	23.8.17		Visited 107 Bde R.F.A. & Army hut where Bomb was dropped on enemy & 2nd wnr – 155/152 Army FA Bde 23 Killed. 27 Wounded C/295 Army Field a Bde. 18 Wdrs. 1 Wounded. A.V. Sect. 2nd DAC. 2 Mules Wounded. Visited 36 M.V.S. Examined 46 horses for Road Evacuation & his service from ADVS. 2 Corps regarding a reach to Nellein? Pm D/298 Army Ps. Verified through Storck VS.	

WAR DIARY
INTELLIGENCE SUMMARY

Army Form C. 2118.

Place	Date	Hour	Summary of Events and Information	Remarks and references to Appendices
ZEVECOTEN	23.8.17 (Cont'd)	3 c.h.15	Visited A.D.V.S. 2 Corps at 10.30pm. arranged for Mallein Sera- Section arrival at 36 h.r.S. to await arrival Mallein Testing Completed. Horses from B/295 R.F.A.'s. 23 Bde TMGS. 2 BdeRE. 30 Division until Mule from A.D.V.S. 2 Corps. Visited 36 hrs.S at 11.30 pm. Stopped non-execution arrangement for testing.	
"	24. 8.17		Sent A.D.V.S 2 Corps - Boxes for Mallein and (Syringes & needles (a storm) Held Conference of Veterinary Officers. Inspected gas alarms. Visited with Mullein (Intradermal Palpebral Method) all sick and doubtful animals at 36 h.r.S. at	
"	25. 8.17		Arrived at 36 h.h.V.S. Inspection. Lorries sent to A.D.V.S-2 Corps. Visited 3 Cav. V. Section. Units at Burgomaster Farm &. 73 Field Ambulance - headquarters with S.A.C. Division + Mar Dept. Tantinschoogoose hook of 3 Cav. V.S. orders for recognition & dispatch M.T.C. Section.	# 3rd Cav Div (Aug 23)

Army Form C. 2118.

WAR DIARY
or
INTELLIGENCE SUMMARY
(Erase heading not required.)

Instructions regarding War Diaries and Intelligence Summaries are contained in F. S. Regs., Part II. and the Staff Manual respectively. Title Pages will be prepared in manuscript.

Place	Date	Hour	Summary of Events and Information	Remarks and references to Appendices
ZEVECOTEN	26.8.17		Conference at office of A.D.V.S. 2nd Corps. Pant. Aircraft Brig. Cavalry/Shelter - P.U.N. - Eye disease - Drilling & foot dressing - Shoeing of horses - at	
"	27.8.17		Visits 3 Br. V. Section. Evacuated 73 cases for consultation - visits 108 Bde R.F.A. at	
	28.8.17		Div in training & II Corps. 2nd Army. Visits A.D.V.S. 2nd and V Corps regarding mountain returns etc. visits 103, 104 & 129 Field Coys R.E. at	
	29.8.17		Visits H. & 5th Brigades R.F.A - 2nd Australian Division & various C.R.A. 2nd Australian Division regarding No. of cavalry patrol at	
	30.8.17		Visits 36a.V.S. issue R.F.a. at headquarters 9M.O's inspection of M.F.A. 2 am.	
	31.8.17		Visits 52nd, 298 Army & A.Bdes Foot drafted during afternoon. Horse check & 12 horses at State 31.8.17.	Shut 28.

CONFIDENTIAL.

War Diary

of

D.A.D.V.S.

24th Division.

From 1-9-17.   To 30-9-17.

Vol. 25.

WAR DIARY
INTELLIGENCE SUMMARY D.A.D.V.S. 24th DIVISION

Army Form C. 2118.

Place	Date	Hour	Summary of Events and Information	Remarks and references to Appendices
ZEVECOTEN	1-9-17		Visited 36th M.V. Section - B/106 - A/109 Bde R.F.A. - 24th Div. Feneral Motors. Forage preservation examined at 36th V Section - One case Strangles found in a horse from 15 Batty - sent to R.F.A. 2 Australian Division. Refuted reverge trade X Corps & notified returning Officer I/c. headquarters QVC.	
"	2-9-17		Visited 36th M.V. Section - H1 Cases preservation examined. Inspected 17th & 43rd Infantry Brigades - also B/106 Bde R.F.A. with Batten Commander.	
"	3-9-17		Inspected 298 Army Field Artillery Bde - Bombs dropped last night on lines of B/298 A.F.A. Bde. 5 mules & 4 horses killed - 1 mule & 9 horses wounded.	
"	4-9-17		Bombs dropped in lines of 24th Divl Signal Company - 9 horses wounded. Visited 36th M.V. Section - A.D.V.S. X Corps - 'Phoned to D.D.V.S. 2 Army regarding Evacuation - 93 cases awaiting same - asked for another day for movements. Returned by D.D.V.S. 2 Army at	

Army Form C. 2118.

WAR DIARY
or
INTELLIGENCE SUMMARY

(Erase heading not required.)

Instructions regarding War Diaries and Intelligence Summaries are contained in F. S. Regs., Part II. and the Staff Manual respectively. Title Pages will be prepared in manuscript.

Place	Date	Hour	Summary of Events and Information	Remarks and references to Appendices
ZEVECOTEN	5-9-17		Visited 36th V Section - 109 Cases awaiting evacuation. Visited 6/106 - Bombardment of high line during night - 1 Killed - 4 wounded. B/107 - 1 wounded. 103 Field Company R.E. 1 Hun officer at	
"	6-9-17		Visited 36th V.S. - 112 Cases awaiting evacuation. Section overfilled. Full up - stopped any further admissions - Visited A + C/107 Bde R.F.A. at	
"	7-9-17		Visited Bth V. Section. - Set train cars sent to 1st Anzac Corps M.V. Sect at	
"	8-9-17		Visited 36th V. Section - 77 Cases evacuation by road - Visited 103, 104, 129 Field Companies R.E., B/107 7 than killed 12 other handed by bombs during night. heavy ulterior at Bruly Division - at	

2449 Wt. W14957/Mg0 750,000 1/16 J.B.C. & A. Forms/C.2118/12.

WAR DIARY or INTELLIGENCE SUMMARY

Army Form C. 2118.

Place	Date	Hour	Summary of Events and Information	Remarks and references to Appendices
ZEVECOTEN	9-9-17		Visited 3 Can. V. Section. Remained all day in Section. Visited No 2 Section D.A.C.	
"	10-9-17		Visited 3 Can V. Section. C/106th Bde R.F.A. and 17th Infantry Brigade. Arrangements to move to Division; wrote instruction book V.O. & G. Animals unable to march. Saw A.A. & QMG regarding horse M3 Can.V.S. to move under orders of Divisional Artillery.	
"	11-9-17		Visited 3 Can.V. Section. A.B.D. 13 Battys 106 Bde R.F.A. Saw A.D.V.S. IX Corps regarding evacuation.	
"	12-9-17		Visited 3 Can.V. Section. Wrote regarding evacuation animals from A.D.S. IX Corps. Remained all animals.	
"	13-9-17		Visited 3 Can.V.S. 92 Can. marched to 1st Anzac Corps. C.C.S. been 1 Sloneth handed on to X Corps M.V. Det. Marching orders from DDVS - 2nd Army.	

WAR DIARY
INTELLIGENCE SUMMARY

Place	Date	Hour	Summary of Events and Information	Remarks and references to Appendices
ZEVECOTEN	13-9-17		(Cont) ADMS. 2nd Army. Saw D.O.M.S. relieving Britain. (O/c. 2nd Division) in Trocar for slurring of C/106 Bn R.F.A. on account of Ophthalmia. CRA notified.	
"	14-9-17		3 O.R.s. V.S. sent to Q.7. A.0.7. (Sheet 27) ADS II Corps notified. Major Standing O.C./106 Bde R.F.A. admitted to account of Ophthalmia - to ADS 15, 23rd & 41st Division - CRA 49th Division. Personnel similar him moved O.9.c O.194 map ref. line.	
"	15-9-17		Division leave ZEVECOTEN. Division arrived MORRIS.	
MORRIS			Capt. M.A. MACGREGOR - ADV returned from leave. of	
"	16-9-17		Whilst 72 Inf. Bde met 163 Field Coy R.E. at	
"	17-9-17		Whilst 73 Field Ambulance - 17th Inf. Bde. In Charge of 17th Bde Amb had B.S. Sharpe medic doing well. of	

WAR DIARY
or
INTELLIGENCE SUMMARY

Army Form C. 2118.

Place	Date	Hour	Summary of Events and Information	Remarks and references to Appendices
MERRIS	18-9-17		Visited 73rd Infantry Bde - 17th I. Base aZ	
"	19-9-17		Visited 129 Field Company R.E. and Cavalry Corps Remount Depôt & a A.D.M.S. G.A.D.M.S. (Lieut. Col. Arthur & 194 Coy att.)	
"	20-9-17		Division H.Q. MORRIS.	
I 34 a 3.7 (Sheet 57c).			Arrived I 34 a 3.7. Notified A D.S. IV Corps.	
			A.D.M.S. to see Divisional Artillery and 194 Coy A.S.C. per Arvil 5	
			9.0. Pte to A.D.S. IV Corps.	
			Reported arrival of ATK & v 3 bde. + S.C.M. 4.6 central - 57e) to ADVS. IV Corps. aZ	
"	21-9-17		Reported personally to ADVS. IV Corps. Visited 36th v.S. gave instructions regarding holding of Stock etc at Section Point. aZ	
"	22-9-17		Conference of A.D.A.D.V.S. at office of ADVS. IV Corps at ETRICOURT. (57e). Visited 36th v. Section. aZ	

2449 Wt. W14957/M90 750,000 1/16 J.B.C. & A. Forms/C.2118/12.

WAR DIARY
or
INTELLIGENCE SUMMARY

Army Form C. 2118.

Place	Date	Hour	Summary of Events and Information	Remarks and references to Appendices
I34 A3.7 (Rus 57c)	23-9-17		Visited 106 and 109 Bn R.F.A at BAPAUME AREA. Saw H.D. (stone) SP 196 Company ASC left behind at ACHIET-LE-PETIT (S49). Driver Duckle O.H. due to P.V.M. Visited 36th V. Section. at	
"	24-9-17		Visited 104 Field Company R.E. - 36 M.V. Section. Saw 129 Field Company R.E. and 73rd Infantry Bde on march. Men at full support. at	
"	25-9-17		Returned G.O.C. Division's RCs who ceased Clipping. Recommended Compulsing Clipping Artones except legs. Saw Horning Levils in March to III Corps. Area: - 24 D.A.C. - 194 Company a.s.c - 106 and 107 Bde (H.Q.C. 212.A.A.) R.F.A. Horses never from A 36th V. Section. Saw part of 72nd Infantry Bde on March.	

WAR DIARY

Army Form C. 2118.

Place	Date	Hour	Summary of Events and Information	Remarks and references to Appendices
I34A3.7 (57°)	26-9-17		Visited N Stretcher Bee.	
"	27-9-17		Left I34A3.7 arrived PERONNE. Sandwich lunch at	
PERONNE	28-9-17		Hearty Conference Veterinary Officers preparation M.F.A. etc. Visited Mobile R.F.a. and A.D.V.S III Corps to view. M.V.S arrived VRAIGNES Rest 82.	
"	29-9-17		Left PERONNE. Arrived NOBESCOURT FARM. Visited 36 M.V.S at VRAIGNES. R.Michelin received from ADVS III Corps Forward inspection by ADVS. 3 Army of Artillery Brigade and 34 A.T.C. at	
Nobescourt Farm K32 c.6. (62°)	30-9-17		Visited 16th Brigade R.F.A and 36th V Section at	

CONFIDENTIAL.

WAR DIARY
of
D.A.D.V.S.

24th DIVISION.

From 1-10-14   To 31-10-14.

Vol. 26.

WAR DIARY
or
INTELLIGENCE SUMMARY DADVS. 24th DIVISION.

Army Form C. 2118.

(Erase heading not required.)

Place	Date	Hour	Summary of Events and Information	Remarks and references to Appendices
NOBESCOURT FARM. K32 Cent. (Mart 62°)	1-10-17		Visited VILLERS-FAUCON (62°) & proceeded LEVERGIES Stn. Two 45th M.V.S. visited B/106 Bde. R.F.A. Senr. N.C.O's gave three affections with Ophthalmia one injection of Argyrol St. Visited 74 Field Ambulance at POEUILLY (62°). Visited 107 Bde R.F.A. A/105 Bde R.F.A. with O/M Captain R.A. Visited 103 Field Company R.E. & Site for Camp & details at HERVILLY.	
"	2-10-17		Visited 3 Cav. F. Section. Inspected 9 Sick arrived - Visited Section 69 M D M C with V.O. Visited Ithenny hinte. — 13/Middlesex Regt - 73 M.G. Coy. — 17th M.G. Coy. — 12/Royal Fusiliers & 1st Royal Fusiliers — 20th Field Company R.E. Checked three sick & 1st R. Fusiliers & 12/Roy Fusiliers - to same found two officers nearly cured & 8 Cat cases in both - Other 15 vacant. Saw AA + QMG regarding Camp for 73rd Infantry Brigade near HERVILLY (62°). Site not good — far from supplies. Returned with same ambulance Army. Saw CRA regarding Ehemy S.P. of D/107 Bde RFA - Ref Horse luata. III Capt. He gave his opinion that annual should figure form 1am - 4pm - When a Red about military waters said it didn't trouble. three horses but had birds more improved upon recovery, of water, 80 percent sodbats and a registration.	

WAR DIARY
or
INTELLIGENCE SUMMARY
(Erase heading not required.)

Army Form C. 2118

Place	Date	Hour	Summary of Events and Information	Remarks and references to Appendices
NOBESCOURT FARM. H32central (62d)			Inspection.	Return Store
	2-10-17	a.m.	Orders received from ADVS. III Corps to instruct all intended for Veterinary Store to him for transmission to Base Veterinary Store. His attention to DVS. Ca. Memo. No 166 dated 28-6-17 which stated he would be divided to division where he submitted to DADVS before transmission to Base Veterinary Store.	
"	3-10-17		Visited 191 Machine Gun Company with Divisional Machine Gun Officer selected and examined horses. 12 shoers for renewed. Inspected 129 Field Company R.E. and 208 Field Company R.E. (34 Division). Mare received to test with Stallion at arrival for overseas. Visits letters by him about perpetual instead 2 horses r12 mules 119, Div. Gun. Coy. with V.O.Ye. Visited 36. M. V. Section. ADVS III Corps asked me upon phone regarding arrival for horses, r inspection by DDVS.	ob/
"	4-10-17		DVS. 3rd Army, ADVS 3rd Corps inspection 4th Divisional Artillery, + DRC. 13 M.V. Section.	ob/

WAR DIARY
or
INTELLIGENCE SUMMARY

Army Form C. 2118

Place	Date	Hour	Summary of Events and Information	Remarks and references to Appendices
NOBESCOURT FARM (K32 Cent)	5-10-17		Held Conference Veterinary Officers & representative of A.F.A 2000. Orders received for Major A. LEANING, AVC to proceed to ABBEVILLE to assume command of No. 5 Veterinary Hospital in relief of Captain W. HALSTEAD. AVC (S.R.). Inspected 1 horse & 10 mules of 191. 2nd Gun Company about to proceed overseas. None arrived here. Mules were "gone sepsic reaction" at	
"	6-10-17		Inspected two chargers of Major General Bols. CB. DSO leaving today for MARSEILLES - Gave certificate of freedom from Contagious infections Disease, which as he had intimated. Animals leaving his Hay. Do J was not possible to shelter them before leaving. Animals attended to and no certificate to Receiving Officer immediately on arrival at MARSEILLES possible. Near arrival can be tendered before embarking. Visited 3rd Aus - Mounted Recorders. Found them French on leaving Division. Annual deworm delinquent. I # Lower are a DADVS.	

WAR DIARY or INTELLIGENCE SUMMARY

Army Form C. 2118

Place	Date	Hour	Summary of Events and Information	Remarks and references to Appendices
NOBESCOURT FARM (K32 Central)	7.10.17		Returned to C Division now here attached to Third Corps. Arrived This Division by breakfast. Preparing documents for typists.	
	8.10.17		Waiting prelim. of	
"	10.10.17.		Saw 24th Division, appointment DADVS in relief of Heys a Leaving.	
"	11.10.17.		Saw ADVS III Corps, was informed at the returns he required from Divisions weekly.	
	12.10.17.		Early conference of V.O.s Subjects been regarding procedure with cases of Contagious diseases, many immediate Evacuation to mobile Vet section. Full case or suspected cases Mange, where a report given, either on Clinical aspects of Mal Case or with the microscope. To be made. Inferiorise A.A. & B.M.G. Division for him statement general health condition of the animals of the Division. Also recommended the making of a Register of melle chandes at 36 M?S. VRAIGNES. The Evacuation of this Chandes is imperative, as Dosvars R.E. personnel are on advience.	

WAR DIARY or INTELLIGENCE SUMMARY

Army Form C. 2118

Place	Date	Hour	Summary of Events and Information	Remarks and references to Appendices
NOBESCOURT FARM. (K.32 Central 62C)	13.10.17.		Inspected Remounts arrived for Division 23 for the units, 26 for Divl. Artillery. Condition of the Remounts satisfactory. They arrived apparently free from sickness & contagious disease. Inspected Coys of 9th & Divl. Train. Ambulance Animals very good. Also inspected range found roads from the Generator to H.F. Pat. Section. Attended Conference of D.V.S. M. Corps.	
"	14.10.17		Inspected Reploning Units, Divl. Headquarters, M.M.P. Lories, also Regimental Transport of 8th Yorks, 1st Royal Fusiliers, 8th East Surreys, 12th Royal Fusiliers, the latter arranged to inspect the Regimental Transport & Ambulance Cars horses found in inspected. 17 Machine Gun Coy, 72 Machine Gun Coy. The latter Coy. has 8 Affiliated Mules. 93 Field Ambulance two suspected mange cases were found in this Division Coy inspected No.1 Coy is attached to this Division Condition the animals The above Units is good.	
"	15.10.17		Inspected the following Units:- 1st Aux. Works Supple - 10 animals Affiliated. Also animals from lines mission by this Unit for Field Artillery Units. Instructions for officer i/c observing Affiliated Mules to be sent.	

1875 W.t. W593/526 1,000,000 4/15 J.B.C. & A. A.D.S.S./Forms/C. 2118.

Army Form C. 2118

WAR DIARY
or
INTELLIGENCE SUMMARY
(Erase heading not required.)

Instructions regarding War Diaries and Intelligence Summaries are contained in F.S. Regs., Part II. and the Staff Manual respectively. Title Pages will be prepared in manuscript.

Place	Date	Hour	Summary of Events and Information	Remarks and references to Appendices
NOBESCOURT FARM. (K32 Central 62ᶜ)	15.10.17. (Cont'd)		9th Royal West Kents. Above Officers & interviews. 72 machine gun coys. 72 Brigade (H.Q.) Headquarters 9th Bn East Surreys. No 224th Signal Coy. The condition generally in these units was good generally.	
"	16.10.17.		Inspected 12th Bn Sherwood Foresters, 1st Bn Northants. 2nd Bn Lincolns, 13th Bn Middlesex, 104 Coy R.E. The Rifle Alec & the latrines on every Inspection arranged & recommendations to M.S. were adopted & substitute animals in 6th Bn Lincolns otherwise general condition satisfactory. Manpower in post	
"	17.10.17.		Staff return rendered to D.M.S. III Corps weekly total corps weekly. Res M officers. V.O.s weekly conference.	
"	18.10.17.		Inspected the following Batteries in Company with Officer Commanding 107 Brigade R.F.A. A/107 Battery, B/107, C/107, D/107. Condition satisfactory. Management generally – Good. 3rd Div. Amm. Col. Condition generally	
"	19.10.17.		Inspected ? elections ? showing good Staff, state management Satisfactory. G.O.C Div/Senior Officers general condition generally Satisfactory. 10 S. Africa Ry R.E. Mis. division	

1875 Wt. W593/826 1,000,000 4/15 J.B.C. & A. A/D.S.S./Forms/C. 2118.

WAR DIARY
or
INTELLIGENCE SUMMARY

(Erase heading not required.)

Army Form C. 2118

Place	Date	Hour	Summary of Events and Information	Remarks and references to Appendices
No. BECOURT FARM. (K.32 Central 62c)	20.10.17.		Inspected the following Batteries. 2/106, 6/106, 2/106, the latter being two a couple of months of allotted horses. In 6/106 Battery 3 inspected horses crew down found & welcome, situation drawn to the consideration of the Brown Warren the late temper of 2/106 Batty.	
	21.10.17.		Inspected. A/106 Battery – Condition for new case peripheral rings, stables. 129 fired by R.E. Condn. 7 animals poor.	
	22.10.17.		Inspected D. Hughes Iron Coy. & 9th Bn. Sussex.	
	23.10.17.		Venue Office Routine.	
	24.10.17.		Inspected the 74 Field Ambulance, arrived practice gallery with extra. Inspected 36 hd. Pot. Section. arranges for a specialist club of antiques. Inspected "Cayeux" area.	
	25.10.17.		Trench Office Routine.	
	26.10.17.		Held A.D.S. VII Corps at R.B. Pot Section. Meet to inspected.	
	27.10.17.		Attended Conference at A.D.S. VII Corps. Interview A.A. & A.M.G. 97 Division.	
	28.10.17.		No. 36 Field Pot. Section inspected. By Director Play Services.	
	29.10.17.		Accompanied Moordonate D.M. & D.M. & Donovan, absorbing areas Sustain to Kelly Camp area.	

Army Form C. 2118

WAR DIARY
or
INTELLIGENCE SUMMARY
(Erase heading not required.)

Place	Date	Hour	Summary of Events and Information	Remarks and references to Appendices
NoBEECOURT FARM (R.32 Central 62c)	20.10.17.		Deputed Annals B. 72 Field Ambulance arranges to appease the Sick Received 94 " Sqn. Cy. horse lines	
"	21.10.17.		Visited Hd. Qt. Section, 3 Br. Ryf. Bde. on case referred by as re Rae, found no intake above one Mecurio Ellatio, 1/R. Rae Trailers. P.Br. Zqr. Trailers 72 Field Ambulance. Inspected 62 Reinsurance Cavalry Men to-gun Myosine apparently free from Contagious disease. The Condition furnished Division is fair. All units are accepting onto status standing. Clipping Horses of properly carefully been carried through being secured in tents - afterwards There have on Increase when Earls Specific ptchiene is Retirement. This disease by pretorio Steyn's Station is Apparently Strong Satisfactory extents. K.A.Okel hys D.A.D.V.S. 9th Division	

CONFIDENTIAL.

WAR DIARY

of

D.A.D.V.S

24th DIVISION.

FROM 1-11-14. To 30-11-14.

VOL. 24

WAR DIARY or INTELLIGENCE SUMMARY

Army Form C. 2118

D.A.D.V.S. 24 DIVISION.

(Erase heading not required.)

Place	Date	Hour	Summary of Events and Information	Remarks and references to Appendices
NORTHCOURT FARM. (K32 c.62 c.)	1.11.17		Visit 1st Bn. & 13th Bn. Royal Fusiliers; also 2nd Bn. Rifle Brigade & 73rd Field Ambulance. In case inspected range were case of scabies & debilitis. All this found in 3rd Rifle Brigade.	
do	2.11.17		Kitting conference of Divisional Vety. Officers.	
do	3.11.17		Attended conference of A.D.V.S. VII Corps.	
do	4.11.17		Inspect with awaiting evacuation at 76 Vet. Y. Section.	
do	5.11.17		Visits 17 "Machine Gun Co" – two cases of suspected mange found isolated. Also visit 8th Bn. Queens.	
do	6.11.17		Inspection horses of Divl. Headquarters also M.M.P. "The Flying Co." and 1st N. Staffs Regt. 1st N. Staffs Regt. 9th Bn. Royal Kents.	
do	7.11.17		Visits 9 Bn. East Surrey Regt. C/106 Batty. Evacuation of the animals ankylosing 12 Machine Gun Coy. A/106 Batty.	
do	8.11.17		Bn. N. Staffs Regt has a number of mydad horses. Inspects sick horses at Lt. Col. Beless that was cavalry evacuation.	
do	9.11.17		Vety. conference of V.O.s of Division. Enters for Run A.F's A2000 Chincored.	
do	10.11.17		Attended conference at office of A.D.V.S. VII Corps.	
do	11.11.17		Visits 106 Bde R.F.A.	
do	12.11.17		Accompanied A.D.V.S. VII Corps who makes inspection of 106 Bde R.F.A.	
do	13.11.17		A.D.V.S. VII Corps inspected animals of 107 Bde R.F.A.	
do	14.11.17		A.D.V.S. VII Corps inspected animals of 8th Wilt. Queens. Col.	

WAR DIARY or INTELLIGENCE SUMMARY

Army Form C. 2118

(Erase heading not required.)

Place	Date	Hour	Summary of Events and Information	Remarks and references to Appendices
Noyelles Rly. (K.29.b.62.)	Nov. 1917		The Senior Veterinary Officer of 5th Irish Division asked permission to visit the Division in order to see the way of operation administration of British Division. This arrangement he states where the Red Xs Section Corps Dipping Bath & some Artillery units.	
do	16.11.17		Weekly Conference DDVS of Division.	
do	17.11.17		Attended A.D.V.S. VII Corps Conference.	
do	18.11.17		A.D.V.S. VII Corps inspected 17" Infy. Bde. also 73" Field Ambulance.	
do	19.11.17		Duties Est. Rly Return inspected with horse ambulance evacuation.	
do	20.11.17			
do	21.11.17		Usual office routine	
do	22.11.17			
do	23.11.17		Conference of Dist V.Os	
do	24.11.17		Attended A.D.V.S. VII Corps Conference.	
do	25.11.17		Sucha 7200 Infantry Bde.	
do	26.11.17		A.D.V.S. VII Corps inspected animals of 72 Infy Bde.	
do	27.11.17		A.D.V.S. VII Corps Inspected animals of 73 Infy Bde.	
do	28.11.17		Inspected D/106, E/106 Div. Batteries.	
do	29.11.17		A.D.V.S. VII Corps inspected animals of 103, 104, 189 Fd. Coy R.E. also 191 Machine Gun Coy, 172 Bn (Pion.) Devon Div.	
do	30.11.17		Conference of DDe V.Os.	

WAR DIARY
or
INTELLIGENCE SUMMARY
(Erase heading not required.)

Army Form C. 2118

The condition of the animals of the Division is good.

Contagious Disease

Mange 7 Cases during the month, all cases are isolated & have had no ill effect inside the Division all except 2 cases returned to the field protight of the month. Leaves were observed than the animals were egyptian.

Ulcerative Cellulitis 11 Cases were evacuated during the month.

Specific Ophthalmia 69 Cases were reported during the month. the best treatment of the month above the invalid number during 13. Treatment is being carried out by injections of Lysol dot. generally tender the cases are injected at the earliest on the symptoms of conjunctivitis & lachrymation are noticed is apparently giving satisfactory results.

B. Halsted Mayr
M.D.V.S. 2nd Division

CONFIDENTIAL.

War Diary

of

D.A.D.V.S

24th Division.

From. 1-12-14.   To. 31-12-14.

Vol. 28.

WAR DIARY
or
INTELLIGENCE SUMMARY D.A.D.V.S. 24th DIVISION.

(Erase heading not required.)

Army Form C. 2118

Place	Date	Hour	Summary of Events and Information	Remarks and references to Appendices
NOYELLESCOURT FARM (K.32.b.62°)	1-12-17		Usual routine. Inspection of animals & grounds of Divisions situated in "A" role. Planned inspection by D.D.R. took a view to the ability of them for obs. than ordinary reserve.	
do	2-12-17		Usual routine.	
do	3-12-17		Definitive list of animals for which officers other ranks should sent in	
do	4-12-17		A. Veterinary Course.	
do	5-12-17		Usual routine.	
do	6-12-17		Usual routine.	
do	7-12-17		Weekly Conference of V.O.'s of Divisions.	
do	8-12-17		Attended A.D.V.S. in Corps Conference. Divisions transferred from VII Corps to Cavalry Corps. Subsequent A.A. + Q.M.G. also held Conference. Generals also verbage during the week. Points on the recent gas arrival very short both Trench stores.	
do	9-12-17			
do	10-12-17		Usual Routine. Inspection of animals.	
do	11-12-17			
do	12-12-17			
do	13-12-17		Proceeded on leave pending to England. Leave granted to 27/12/17. Capt. J.H. Davies A.V.C. O.C. 36 M.O.B. Vet Section performs duty.	

Army Form C. 2118

WAR DIARY
or
INTELLIGENCE SUMMARY

(Erase heading not required.)

D.A.D.V.S. 24th DIVISION

Instructions regarding War Diaries and Intelligence Summaries are contained in F.S. Regs., Part II. and the Staff Manual respectively. Title Pages will be prepared in manuscript.

Place	Date	Hour	Summary of Events and Information	Remarks and references to Appendices
NOBESCOURT FARM (K3ab) (29°)	14.12.17		} Usual Routine	
	15.12.17			
	16.12.17			
	17.12.17			
	18.12.17			
	19.12.17			
	20.12.17			
	21.12.17			
	22.12.17			
	23.12.17			
	24.12.17			
	25.12.17			
	26.12.17			
	27.12.17			
	28.12.17			
do	29.12.17		Inspected Division on return from line. Superintended in hos. Pit section	
	30.12.17		Arranges for reinvestigation from units. Pass of Mumps (Helihourne swine.)	
	31.12.17		Usual Routine	

The general condition of animals of the Division is very good. All animals have been clipped all over except legs, which went recently a scrape and mount remainder of range. Those affected away to were well prepared. Coats are not so long in proportion as long as temperature keeps mild. All animals are shod till further orders.

WAR DIARY or INTELLIGENCE SUMMARY

Army Form C. 2118

DADVS 2th DIVISION

March During the month 3 Deaths of Horses have been reported from Groups. The Losses generally in Hospital units who need remounting in any one unit being 3.

Medical Casualties Have come from accepted duty for recent.

Opthalmic Opthalmia The chances shown a marked increase following to last two weeks month, coinciding with the climatic Conditions — Foot & Mouth. Several new cases have been received during the month. These represented renewal being standing cases showing marked inflammation changes in the eye. It was not to satisfactory like the mortality of some units the slight loss liable to occur in large hunts to be relieved but there seems only to lack accommodation at Retn Sec Section.

K Hatchah Major
DADVS 2d R Division

CONFIDENTIAL.

WAR DIARY.
of
D.A.D.V.S

24th DIVISION.

FROM. 1-1-18.   To 31-1-18.

Vol. 29.

Army Form C. 2118.

WAR DIARY
or
INTELLIGENCE SUMMARY   D.A.D.V.S. 24th DIVISION
(Erase heading not required.)

Place	Date	Hour	Summary of Events and Information	Remarks and references to Appendices
NOYES COURT FARM (K 32 b Sheet 62B)	1.1.18		Visit 107 Bde R.F.A. Condition generally very good. 15 Cases of specific Ophthalmia in lines. Two cases of suspected mange in C/107 Battery.	
do	2.1.18		Visited 16 Bde. R.G.A. attached to Division. 132 Buty horses – condition from + approaching fair from thin animals. 113 Baty. a large number of thin horses – specific ophth. mange. Evacuations for this Arma numerous – Animal Protection taken – reported to D.D.V.S. Corps. Visit 72 Field Ambulance – Condition very fair.	
do	3.1.18		Visited B/106, C/106, D/106 Batteries – Condition generally very fair. Specific ophthalmia – all these batteries have a large number of cases of specific ophthalmia. The condition of the animals is mainly due to the eye trouble. In other instance healthier appearance not apparent. Suggested treatment supplied as before any intervening month.	
do	4.1.18		V.D's work continues.	
do	5.1.18		Inspected 17th Machine Gun Coy. Condition very good. The best head of several seen of late. Horses transferred for this Ophthalmia selection by him acquires the change – although the whole thing remains firm – horses shown no sign of pressure. (Stamps of 3rd Bn Rifle Brigade – Colchester)	
do	6.1.18		Visited 8 Bn. Buffs – Condition good, also 3rd Bn Rifle Brigade – Colchester. Usual Routine	
do	7.1.18		Visited No. 35 Bde Battalion inspected remounts arriving Trainload 65 at Base	
do	8.1.18		Inspected 47 Remounts arriving by train at PERONNE	
do	9.1.18		Visits 72 Machine Gun Coy. Condition generally good.	

WAR DIARY or INTELLIGENCE SUMMARY

Army Form C. 2118.

DADVS. 24th DIVISION.

Place	Date	Hour	Summary of Events and Information	Remarks and references to Appendices
Nobescourt Farm (M 32 b) (62d)	10.1.18		Inspected 1st Bn Royal Fusiliers - Condition good. also 12th Bn Royal Fusiliers - Condition good. 73rd Field Ambulance - Condition any good. Trucks & taking horseshoes.	
do	11.1.18		V.O's weekly conference	
do	12.1.18		Visited No 30 Field Vet. Section.	
do	13.1.18		Inspected animals of 104 Field Coy R.E. Condition fair. except for bell animals one.	
do			Case pneumonia isolated.	
do	14.1.18		Inspected animals of 103 Field Coy R.E. Condition good. Proving unsatisfactory.	
do	15.1.18		Inspected animals of D.A.C. No 2 Echelon. Saw Colonel animals effectively kept.	
do			Visited weekly pet through Cav. Corps Dipping Bath.	
do	16.1.18		Inspected 17 Remount recently from PERONNE.	
do	17.1.18		Office Routine	
do	18.1.18		V.O's weekly conference.	
do	19.1.18		Visited No 30 F.V.S. & D/105 Batteries. saw Staff Capt. and new fodder.	
do			Line troop fit - now landing. Condition.	
do	20.1.18		Attended Cav. Corps HQ & interview with D.D.V.S.	
do	21.1.18		Visit 1st Bn Queens, 1st Bn W. Staffords, also 8th Bn Royal W. Kents & A/106 Bath., also 9th Bn East Surreys.	
do	22.1.18		Visited No 30 Vet Hot Section	
do	23.1.18		Arranged for ascertaining of specific ophthalmia cases to H.Q. Veterinary. also	
do			arrange for removing of 1 team trangs' cases advised through M.O. by	
do	24.1.18		Inspected Officer's ophthalmia case and and return	

WAR DIARY
or
INTELLIGENCE SUMMARY   DADVS 2nd DIVISION

Army Form C. 2118.

Place	Date	Hour	Summary of Events and Information	Remarks and references to Appendices
Nobescourt Farm (K.32.b.6.2.c.)	25.1.18		V.O.'s Weekly Conference	
do	26.1.18		Visited Mob. Vet. Section, Lepröle & "Nyrolles" R.E.	
do	27.1.18		Office Routine.	
do	28.1.18		Examined cases of specific ophthalmia at M.V.S.	
do	29.1.18		A suspected case of specific lymphangitis reported by V.O. in a horse of M/106 Bde. Examined animal. Swabs taken & despatched to N°.5 Veterinary Hospital for microscopic examination. Await preparation of serum & later injection.	
do	30.1.18		Lymphangitis of Divisional Train. Condition myford suskes shong.	
do	31.1.18		Confident. Suspects ophthalmia cases at M.V.S. for section.	

K Whitehead Major
DADVS 2nd Division

CONFIDENTIAL.

Vol 30

WAR DIARY

of

D.A.D.V.S.

24th DIVISION.

FROM 1-2-18. To 28-2-18.

VOL 30.

D.A.D.V.S.,
24th DIVISION.
No. V3957
Date 1-2-18

Army Form C. 2118.

WAR DIARY
or
INTELLIGENCE SUMMARY

(Erase heading not required.)

DADVS. 34th DIVISION.

Instructions regarding War Diaries and Intelligence Summaries are contained in F. S. Regs., Part II. and the Staff Manual respectively. Title Pages will be prepared in manuscript.

Place	Date	Hour	Summary of Events and Information	Remarks and references to Appendices
NOBESCOURT FARM.	1.2.18		V.O. Conference	
Do	2.2.18		Inspected horses of 129 Field Co RE +12"The Skinners" Forester	
Do	3.2.18		Inspected horses of 113 Hy RGA. Saw DDVS. Cav. Corps with reference to mules	
Do	4.2.18		Various camps & Vet Lab, journey to the west	
Do	5.2.18		Visited HQ Veterans Inspected horses, sundry conferences	
Do	6.2.18		Head Quarters	
Do	7.2.18		Interior economy of Brit Headquarters & 5th Legage Coy	
Do	8.2.18		Inspected Remount Annexe of PERONNE Field mover in duration	
Do	9.2.18		V.Os. Conference	
Do	10.2.18		Inspected animals 5/107 Am. T.M.B.	
Do	11.2.18		Inspected animals of 178th Bn A.F.A.	
Do	12.2.18		Visits MO Veterinary hospitals, attended to sundry inspection of	
Do	13.2.18		Brit Cavan Colmiers	
Do	14.2.18		Visits 17 Inf Bde.	
Do	15.2.18		Inspected animals of 3 Inspected + 10 K Br British hospitals	
Do	16.2.18		On duty with related inspected animals country evacuation	
Do	17.2.18		V.O. Conference	
Do	18.2.18		Annual Returns	
Do	19.2.18		Inspected animals 97 & 8 Inf Bde	
Do	20.2.18		On the L.9. But Vet on	

WAR DIARY or INTELLIGENCE SUMMARY

Army Form C. 2118.

DADVS 24th DIVISION

(Erase heading not required.)

Place	Date	Hour	Summary of Events and Information	Remarks and references to Appendices
NOBESCOURT FARM	19.3.18		Issued Divl Orders.	
do	20.3.18		Inspected animals 143rd Bty. R.G.A.	
do	21.3.18		Had Bath at Cobru. Inspected animals of Ammunition	
do	22.3.18		V.O. Sundry Complaints	
do	23.3.18		Visited MR Staden and DDVS Cav Corps.	
do	24.3.18		Inspected Dby Batt 262/07 Bdes.	
do	25.3.18		Office Routine.	
do	26.3.18		42 Jrses moved from area on 25th. March to CORBIE. VO accompanied Bde.	
do	27.3.18		Visited Posts Stations 165 Bde R.F.A.	
do	28.3.18		MTH 1st Section, 17 Jrses sent help men on mot. for BOVES AREA.	

Conditions: Animals – Good.
Hay – Issues are continuing. Fodder in middle – class is much of inferior
Frost bitten – Burnt out Regt.
Office & Billets are the Muddier Officers Cross. High ground for them dry.
Health of the trucks – strong, but would say to save men entertd for the
Cold Showers.

W. McMahon Capt
DADVS 24th Division

CONFIDENTIAL.

Vol 3

> D.A.D.V.S.,
> 24th DIVISION.
> No. V.8
> Date. 9-4-18

War Diary

of

D.A.D.V.S

24th Division

From 1-3-18.   To 31-3-18.

Vol. 31.

Army Form C. 2118.

WAR DIARY
or
INTELLIGENCE SUMMARY.
(Erase heading not required.)

DADVS 24th DIVISION.

Place	Date	Hour	Summary of Events and Information	Remarks and references to Appendices
NoBEscourt FARM.	1.3.18		VOs weekly conference. Divisions awaiting relief by 66 Division.	
do	2.3.18		"G" "Q" branch of Division moved to METZ au COURT. Depots etcetera to FLAMICOURT.	
FLAMICOURT	3.3.18		Transport Lines arrived at DEVISE, MONTECOURT, MONCHY LAGACHE. 36 Mob Vet Section YRAIGNES.	
do	4.3.18		Visit Mob Vet Section with a view to their moving with own Hus to 66 Div area.	
do	5.3.18		Mob. Vet Section moved to BOUVINCOURT. Heavy ROICEL to VRAIGNES.	
do	6.3.18		Leave routine.	
do	7.3.18		Inspected 36 Remounts arriving by rail at La Chapelette.	
do	8.3.18		VOs weekly conference.	
do	9.3.18		Divisional Horse Show XIX Corps form Cav Corps.	
do	10.3.18		Leave Routine.	
do	11.3.18		Visits AA&QMG reference my being after from Transport Lines two horses had succumbed to heats accommodation at MEREAUCOURT. Inspected animals of Hy. Tp. Sec.	
do	12.3.18		Inspects of 107 Bde RFA as a number of sore shoulders had occurred.	
do	13.3.18		Rifle of Div. H.Qrs moved to BOUVINCOURT. 36 Mob Vet Section move to TERTRY with Rations it ma Central for ae Transport Lines. Railhead ROISEL with Attention Rathead at La Chapelette.	
BOUVINCOURT	14.3.18		Attended DDR. 5th Army Inspection for erecting Inoculation for crating glanders in Army into only Horses	

WAR DIARY or INTELLIGENCE SUMMARY

Army Form C. 2118.

DADVS 24th DIVISION

Place	Date	Hour	Summary of Events and Information	Remarks and references to Appendices
BOUVINCOURT	15.3.18		Inspected 106 & 107 Btys R.F.A.	
do	16.3.18		Visited 66 Divisional Mob. Vet. Sect. with ADVS XIX Corps. The bought 36 Mob. Vet. Section slowed overripe VRAIGNES on account of Zeppelin being at BERNES.	
do	17.3.18		Inspected Div. Machine Batt'n animals.	
do	18.3.18		A.D.V.S. XIX Corps accompanied to Corps Horseshow, inspected 26th Div. Artillery.	
do	19.3.18		Visited Mob. Vet. Section & 129 Coy R.E.	
do	20.3.18		Inspected 17th Inf. Bde.	
do	21.3.18		Visited 13th Glencorlie Regt (Pioneer Bn of 24 Division) at Beauvois & also Mob. Vet. Section. Bombarded heavy about Bern also being shelled. In consultation with "Q" Mob. Vet. Section ordered to move to BRIE on following day along with Divisional Train. Mob. Vet. Section moved to BRIE after pulling on horses at La Chapellette at 4pm. Mob. Vet. Section ordered on to the Somme to Villers Carbonel. O.C. instructed to move with the Divisional Train where situation is that would look instructions to hqrs.	
do	22.3.16.		V.O.'s rail crossings informed that Mob. Vet. Section moved alongside forward with Div. Train that sick numbers animals were to rail truck with the Empty Supply wagons returning from trucks. Div. Hdqrs at BRIE.	

Army Form C. 2118.

WAR DIARY
or
INTELLIGENCE SUMMARY.
(Erase heading not required.)

Place	Date	Hour	Summary of Events and Information	Remarks and references to Appendices
BRIE	23.3.18.		Div¹ Hq⁵ moved to MARCHLEPOT Afn. to HALLU. Mob. Vet. Section to LIHONS.	
HALLU.	24.3.18.		Div¹ Hq⁵ move to ROSIERES. Mob. Vet. Section to HARBONNIERS.	
ROSIERES.	25.3.18.		Div¹ Hq⁵ move to DEMUIN. Mob. Vet. Section to THENNES.	
do	26.3.18		Visits Mob. Vet. Section. OC reported that not many animals were coming in but that horses being no. sufficient - a remounting by Maun.	
do	27.3.18		Usual routine	
do	28.3.18.		Div¹ Hq⁵ move to CASTEL.	
do	29.3.18.		Div¹ Hq⁵ move to COTTENCHY.	
do	30.3.18		Chance meeting Ipswich.	
do	31.3.18		The animals shewn condition were during the retreat. Hay & came Ychken Animals suffered. All wagons were overloaded, unitd aid not ret'n numerous requests that its accumulation during the stationary warfare. 104 Horses & 143 mules were killed wn 5 th detatcn. All bounces Animals Vet. Corea broken. During the period 21/3/18 to 31/3/18. 62 Animals from Corea etc. Whitehead Major DADVS 2n Div⁰	

CONFIDENTIAL.

War Diary.

of.

D.A.D.V.S.

24th DIVISION.

FROM 1-4-18.   TO 30-4-18.

Vol. 32.

Army Form C. 2118.

WAR DIARY
or
INTELLIGENCE SUMMARY.
(Erase heading not required.)

DADVS 24th DIVISION

Place	Date	Hour	Summary of Events and Information	Remarks and references to Appendices
COTTENCHY	1.4.18.		36 Mob. Vet. Sections located BUYON nr SALEUX	
do	2.4.18.		Usual Routine.	
do	3.4.18.		D.H.Q. moved to BOVES at 10 a.m. Mob. Vet. Section to VERS.	
do	4.4.18.		D.H.Q. moved to BOUTILLERIE, S.E. AMIENS at 8 p.m. Infantry relieved evacuated at LONGEAU prior to proceeding to SALEUX	
do	5.4.18.		Station for rest area ST VALERY-SUR-SOMME.	
do	6.4.18.		As 96th Advanced Artillery was moving in the area 36 Mob. Vet. Section has been known in the NCO, 13 O.R. along with necessary equipment ats the to attack by OC, Mob Vet. Section to proceed with remainder of Division to rest area. This detachment to be attached to 96 Coy A.S.C. All transport marches through to rest area. D.H.Q. moved to ST VALERY-SUR-SOMME.	
ST VALERY sur SOMME	7.4.18.		Office routine. Division came under XVIII Corps.	
do	8.4.18.		Wrote A.D.V.S. XVIII Corps Divisional Artillery now to Pix area troops. Divisional Transport arrived ST VALERY area. Detachment of 36 Mob Vet Section located at ARREST. Capt. Towsee taken ill on leave injured & taken to 96 Coy A.S.C. to take over & make necessary arrangements for the evacuation of Such animals sent to the M.V.S. detachment, by return to No 14 V. Hospital. ABBEVILLE.	
do	9.4.18.		Visited Mob Vet Section detachment at ARREST, & 17 Supplu along 96 Coy A.S.C.	

Army Form C. 2118.

WAR DIARY
or
INTELLIGENCE SUMMARY.
(Erase heading not required.)

DADVS. 24th DIVISION

Place	Date	Hour	Summary of Events and Information	Remarks and references to Appendices
ST VALERY-SUR-SOMME	10.4.18		Inspected 24 Machine Gun Bn animals	
do	11.4.18		Divisional Artillery moved to SOREL & WANEL. 36 Mob. Vet Section located at WANEL. Inspected 7th Field Ambulance animals	
do	12.4.18		Visited M.V. Detachment	
do	13.4.18		Office routine	
do	14.4.18		Visited 36 Mob. Vet. Section at WANEL, also inspected Divisional Artillery animals	
do	15.4.18		Office routine	
do	16.4.18		D.H.Q. moved from ST VALERY to LATHIEULOYE. Divisional Am Artillery	
do	17.4.18		Moved by train. Mob Vet Detachment placed at VALHUON	
do	18.4.18		Office routine	
LATHIEULOYE	19.4.18		36 Mob. Vet Section at RAMECOURT with Divisional Artillery. Visited Mob. Vet Detachment	
do	20.4.18		Moved M.V. Detachment to Divisional sick animals admitted to 36 M.V. Section	
do	21.4.18		Inspected 1st Bn. M. Staffs annual Condition very poor. Arranged for animals to be evacuated & improvements to be made in the horse management. Artillery moved to LE CAUROY area. 36 M.V. Section moved to LECAUROY. FREVENT had as Railhead. Mob. Vet Detachment moved to evacuate sick animals to First Army Collecting Station at RAMECOURT	

Army Form C. 2118.

WAR DIARY
or
INTELLIGENCE SUMMARY

(Erase heading not required)

DADVS. 24th DIVISION.

Place	Date	Hour	Summary of Events and Information	Remarks and references to Appendices
LA THIEULOYE	22.4.18		Inspected animals of 8th Bn Queens Regt, also 1st Bn Royal Fusiliers.	
do	23.4.18		Inspected animals of 9th Bn Sussex Regt, 103 Coy R.E., 8th Bn R.W. Kents, 9th Bn R.E. Sussex.	
do	24.4.18		Visited M.R.N. Staff.	
do	25.4.18		Inspected animals of 3 Bn. Rifle Brig.	
do	26.4.18		Office routine.	
do	27.4.18		Visited 35 Inst. Vet. Section	
do	28.4.18		Office routine.	
do	29.4.18		Visited 8th Bn Queens Regt.	
do	30.4.18		Office routine.	

B. Malcolm Major
DADVS. 24th Division

Army Form C. 2118.

24

WAR DIARY
or
INTELLIGENCE SUMMARY.
(Erase heading not required)

DADVS 24th DIVISION   Vol 33

Instructions regarding War Diaries and Intelligence Summaries are contained in F.S. Regs., Part II. and the Staff Manual respectively. Title pages will be prepared in manuscript.

Place	Date	Hour	Summary of Events and Information	Remarks and references to Appendices
LA THIEULOYE	1-5-18		Divisional Headquarters at LA THIEULOYE. Detachments had Vety Section at VALHUON. 36 Mob. Vet. Section at LE CAUROY.	
do	2-5-18		Division now formed only of 3rd Cav. Division. Detached 9th & 10th Brig. moved to BARLIN.	
do	3-5-18		DHQ moved to SAINS-EN-GOHELLE.	
SAINS-EN-GOHELLE	4-5-18		Div Artillery came with division from Lucia locate - one Vet Sect SAINS-EN-GOHELLE. One Vet ABLAIN-ST NAZAIRE. DAC at FOSSE 10. MARQUOILETTE. 36 Rd. Vet Section placed at FOSSE 10. Formerly to locate Transport lines Division. 17 Inf.Bde hqrs - LES BREBIS, 72 Inf.Bde hqrs - FOSSE 10. 73 Inf.Bde hqrs LES BREBIS, Div. Train - BARLIN. Detachment 9 M.V.S. at home MVS. opens MVS at Fosse 10.	
do	5-5-18			
do	6-5-18		Arrangements made to pick mounted animals Vet Horses over to VE?s at BARLIN. Inst. Vet Section & Horps VE? at BARLIN Orderlies 9/C & D Sect animals feir Mob. Vet Section temporary returns of sick horses dve.	
do	7-5-18		Insp. both Mob. Vet Sections C/V1 & MVS Brigade	
do	8-5-18			
do	9-5-18		Inspected Evening VC & Rackine Gun Coy.	

Army Form C. 2118.

WAR DIARY
or
INTELLIGENCE SUMMARY.
(Erase heading not required.)

DADVS 24th DIVISION.

Place	Date	Hour	Summary of Events and Information	Remarks and references to Appendices
SAINS-EN-GOHELLE	10.5.18		Rear Headqrs. Division formed at GOUY-SERVINS consisting of "A" & "Q". Bobola. DADOS. Dist. Employment Coy. Truck Reserve.	
do	11.5.18		Attended A.D.V.S. Conference. Graded M.V.S.	
do	12.5.18.		Inspected 73 Field Ambulance animals.	
do	13.5.18		Inspected animals of D/107 & B/107 Batteries	
do	14.5.18		Inspected 72 Suffolks animals	
do	15.5.18		Inspected 72 Field Ambulance animals, animals awaiting casting from M.V.S.	
do	16.5.18		Inspected 48 Regimental First arrivals at Bird Farm for distribution	
do	17.5.18		Visited kennels Divisional Run also M.V.S.	
do	18.5.18		Visited the Pulhams Gun Ammunition storing arrangements for an Shoeing Smith Battle & horse.	
do	19.5.18		Inspected animals 9/3 Suffolks.	
do	20.5.18		Inspected with ADVS XVIII Corps animals PSC & D Reserve 106 Fd.	
do	21.5.18		Inspected animals N°1 & Selection DAC.	
do	22.5.18		Inspected 124 Reinforcements at N° 2 Selection DAC.	
do	23.5.18.		Inspected animals 9/103 & 9/104 Field Coys RE	

WAR DIARY
or
INTELLIGENCE SUMMARY.

Army Form C. 2118.

Place	Date	Hour	Summary of Events and Information	Remarks and references to Appendices
SAINS-EN-GOHELLE	24.5.18		Inspection arrangements of 24 Div Train.	
do	25.5.18		Inspection arrangements 9/1/7 Coy R.E.	
do	26.5.18		Visits 1/107 A/107 Batteries	
do	27.5.18		Attended cadre Parade 9/2DR 2/Army	
do	28.5.18		Visits M.S.	
do	29.5.18		Inspection arrangement 24th Signal Coy., DDVS, 2/Army visits 26 Inst.	
do	30.5.18		Medical	
do	31.5.18		General Routine	
			Contain Humada to for Enquiry regarding Bug Colin Skepys.	
			Contagious diseases Specific Epthotoma a few cases during month. 2 gunshot sin	
			range 3 cases occurring during month.	
			Wounds 15.	
			A. Mitchell Major	
			DADVS 24th Division	

CONFIDENTIAL

Vol 34

War Diary.
of
D.A.D.V.S.

24th Division.

From. 1-6-18.   To. 30-6-18.

Vol. 34

D.A.D.V.S.,
24th DIVISION.
No V.300
Date 12-7-18

WAR DIARY
INTELLIGENCE SUMMARY

Army Form C. 2118.

DADVS. 24th DIVISION.

Place	Date	Hour	Summary of Events and Information	Remarks and references to Appendices
SAINC-EN-GOHELLE	1/6/18		Inspected animals of B.Sup Coln + No 2 Section DAC	
do	2/6/18		Rode Ze Ligne Coy inspected animals of M/4 Trench Rs + 24th trench Lun Rs	
do	3/6/18		Inspected animals of Nos 1 & 3 Sections DAC	
do	4/6/18		Rest de Mot. Mt. Sect. Inspected animals awaiting transfer	
do	5/6/18		Inspected animals of 107 Rue RFA	
do	6/6/18		Inspected animals of 112 the Howitzer Brigade + 17 Sup Coln looked into billet	
do	7/6/18		Inspected animals B/106 Bde RFA	
do	8/6/18		Conference inspected animals of the Brit. Train	
do	9/6/18		Inspected R.A. Vet. Section	
do	10/6/18		Inspected animals of C/106 + B/106 Proceeding to Field Co RE	
do	11/6/18		Inspected animals of 9/103 Field AFO Rodea Exhibition	
do	12/6/18		Inspected animals of D/106 Bn AFO	
do	13/6/18		The notice Mille Molyea Coy	
do	14/6/18		No. Conference Rode to the Reception to of infirmerie & ordern	
do	15/6/18		Rode Colliere ard pontoon	
do	16/6/18		Rode the Ze section inspected animals awaiting Evacuation	
do	17/6/18		Rode routine B/153	
do	18/6/18		Office routine Batt RFA rode to Z.2 Station	

Army Form C. 2118.

WAR DIARY
or
INTELLIGENCE SUMMARY.
(Erase heading not required.)

DADVS 24th DIVISION

Place	Date	Hour	Summary of Events and Information	Remarks and references to Appendices
SAINS-EN-GOHELLE			Inspected 1st Sept Cy	
do	16/9/18		Saeth Pier Transports 3rd R Dn	
do	19/9/18		Inspected animals of 73rd Inf Bde	
do	20/9/18			
do	21/9/18		V.O.S Conference Offices routine	
do	22/9/18		heitse MOI Rt Section Inspected animals awaiting Evacuation	
do	23/9/18		heitse 3/97 75th Bdes R.F.A. Inspected Animals 97 & 107 Batys R.F.A.	
do	24/9/18		Inspected Mob Vet Section 24th Divne Cy	
do	25/9/18			
do	26/9/18			
do	27/9/18		Routine	
do	28/9/18			
do	29/9/18			
do	30/9/18			

W. Hickman Major
DADVS 24th Division

D.D. & L., London, E.C.
(A8004) Wt. W1717/M1131. 750,000 5/17 Sch. 52 Forms/C2118/14

CONFIDENTIAL

WAR DIARY
of
D.A.D.V.S.

24th DIVISION

FROM 1-7-18. To 31-7-18.

VOL. 35.

Army Form C. 2118.

WAR DIARY
or
INTELLIGENCE SUMMARY.

(Erase heading not required.)

DADVS 24th DIVISION.

Place	Date	Hour	Summary of Events and Information	Remarks and references to Appendices
SAINS EN GOHELLE	1.7.18		Went routine inspections of animals. Condition of horses and mules in units that lost animals on arrival of infers has very much improved owing to the efforts	
do	2.7.18			
	3.7.18		available as to rest of refugees. Going to the effects	
	4.7.18			
	5.7.18		to animals seen evacuate to Details now of contagious diseases	
	6.7.18			
	7.7.18			
	8.7.18			
SAINS EN GOHELLE	9.7.18		Went routine inspections. Made personals remounts + Details.	
	10.7.18			
	11.7.18			
do	12.7.18			
	13.7.18			
do	14.7.18		1 horse during the period.	
	15.7.18			
	16.7.18			
SAINS EN GOHELLE	17.7.18		Routine inspections. 1 horse evacuated. The one casualty. The source of infection could not be traced. Condition of the animals	
do	18.7.18			
	19.7.18			
	20.7.18		is good. Going improved afternoon specially 1/5 W Rid of	
	21.7.18		Truly Greenwood. Going worth the Animal and their hair	
do	22.7.18			
	23.7.18		sufficient training.	

Army Form C. 2118.

WAR DIARY
or
INTELLIGENCE SUMMARY.
(Erase heading not required.)

D.A.D.V.S. 24th DIVISION.

Place	Date	Hour	Summary of Events and Information	Remarks and references to Appendices
SAINS EN GOHELLE	24.7.18		Routine inspections. Evacuations animals - 1 Horse, 1 debil.	
do.	25.7.18		2 Mention Casualties.	
do.	26.7.18		The several post bring down to animals	
do.	27.7.18		is comparatively small. Horses of Batteries doing little another	
do.	28.7.18		exercise.	
do.	29.7.18			
do.	30.7.18		Location of new units from 2 Brigades very close.	
do.	31.7.18		These include grenades evacuations during present mo 37.	

W. Holden Major
D.A.D.V.S. 24th Division

CONFIDENTIAL.

War Diary

of

D.A.D.V.S.

24th DIVISION

From 1-8-18.   To 31-8-18.

Vol 36.

Army Form C. 2118.

WAR DIARY
or
INTELLIGENCE SUMMARY.

(Erase heading not required.)

DADVS. 24th DIVISION

Instructions regarding War Diaries and Intelligence Summaries are contained in F. S. Regs., Part II. and the Staff Manual respectively. Title pages will be prepared in manuscript.

Place	Date	Hour	Summary of Events and Information	Remarks and references to Appendices
SAINS-EN-GOHELLE	1.8.18		Routine inspection of units of Division. Inmates evacuated from Division	
	2.8.18		inspection of units. Scabies range 1. Ulceration Cellulitis 2.	
	3.8.18			
	4.8.18			
	5.8.18		Anaerobic (Purps) ophthalmia 5.	
	6.8.18			
	7.8.18			
SAINS-EN-GOHELLE	8.8.18		Routine inspection. Animals evacuated from Division. Horses - 15. Mules 4.	
	9.8.18		Greatest Mount Casualties - Scabies 3. Horses 3. Mules 7.	
	10.8.18		Conf. Horse 17. Sub. 4. Sarcoptic Mange - 1.	
	11.8.18			
	12.8.18		ADVS VIII Corps Conference re Cattle Clipping. Returns for Drawers.	
	13.8.18			
	14.8.18		ADVS Rt. Section moved from FORCE 10 to BOUVIGNY - BOYEFFLES. All	
	15.8.18		36 Mob. Vet. Section	
	16.8.18		Moi Vans moved from FORCE 10. Received of enemy shelling	
SAINS-EN-GOHELLE	17.8.18		Routine Inspections. Animals evacuated from Division. Horses - 6	
	18.8.18		Mules - 7. No infection of Contagious disease.	
	19.8.18			
	20.8.18			
	21.8.18			
	22.8.18			
SAINS-EN-GOHELLE	23.8.18		Routine inspections. Animals evacuated. Horses 12. Mules 2.	
	24.8.18		Sarcoptic mange 1. Ulceration Cellulitis 1.	
	25.8.18			
	26.8.18			
	27.8.18			
	28.8.18			
	29.8.18			
	30.8.18			
	31.8.18			

Horse Mastership
Condition of animals

Army Form C. 2118.

WAR DIARY
or
INTELLIGENCE SUMMARY.
(Erase heading not required.)

DADVS. 24th DIVISION

Place	Date	Hour	Summary of Events and Information	Remarks and references to Appendices
			Creation of Kennels out the whole - force Horsemanship - indifferent, though young officers & NCO know at time attend course of instruction. I try & give them any opportunity. Farriery in field animals. The Life Veal Officer comes very recent to the Laundaing Pokie took on Service. Farmers Manuals to returns to the animals, their ration & ration Book took after anim's ts experience. Spring Regimen Creation of Reserve of Reserve founds. Field Veterinary Sections. Personal Veterinary officer field today into yesterday on Leave. Et Con by day when Sn. Vet. hospital town was become "static", make their transport useless for further service.	A.Baldwin Major DADVS 24 Division

CONFIDENTIAL.

War Diary

of

D.A.D.V.S.

24th DIVISION.

From. 1-9-18.   To. 30-9-18.

Vol. 37.

Army Form C. 2118.

WAR DIARY
~~INTELLIGENCE SUMMARY~~ D.A.D.V.S. 24th DIVISION.

(Erase heading not required.)

Place	Date	Hour	Summary of Events and Information	Remarks and references to Appendices
SAINS-EN-GOHELLE	1.9.18		Usual Routine inspection of animals & units. 17 Horses & 9 mules Evacuated. Three inclined scares of anaphic mange.	
do	2.9.18			
	3.9.18			
	4.9.18			
	5.9.18			
do	6.9.18		Routine inspections. 6 animals evacuated including one case of suspected mange.	
	7.9.18			
	8.9.18			
	9.9.18			
	10.9.18			
	11.9.18			
	12.9.18			
do	13.9.18		Routine inspections. 21 animals evacuated during week.	
	14.9.18			
	15.9.18			
	16.9.18			
	17.9.18			
	18.9.18			
	19.9.18			
do	20.9.18		Routine Inspections. Conference with D.D.V.S. VIII Corps re Curlee clipping & taking measures to check no suspected.	
	21.9.18			
	22.9.18			
	23.9.18		Special in view further questions. 18 animals evacuated	
	24.9.18		including 2 cases of anaphic mange.	
	25.9.18			
	26.9.18			

Army Form C. 2118.

WAR DIARY
or
INTELLIGENCE SUMMARY.

(Erase heading not required.)

D.A.D.V.S. 24th DIVISION.

Place	Date	Hour	Summary of Events and Information	Remarks and references to Appendices
SAINS-EN-GOHELLE	27.9.18		V.Os. Conferences reference M.V.S. Officers Drivers taking on a/c. reflex.	
	28.9.18		Visited 58th Division reference No. 36 Mot. Vet. Section.	
	29.9.18		No. 36 Mot. Vet. Section moved to PERNIN.	
	30.9.18		Division moved to LUCHEUX.	

W. Fladden Major
D.A.D.V.S. 24th Divl.

CONFIDENTIAL

War Diary
of
D.A.D.V.S.

24th Division

From 1-10-18.   To 31-10-18.

Vol. 38.

D.A.D.V.S.,
24th DIVISION.
No. V554
Date 2-11-18

Army Form C. 2118.

WAR DIARY
or
INTELLIGENCE SUMMARY.
(Erase heading not required.)

DADVS 24th DIVISION

Place	Date	Hour	Summary of Events and Information	Remarks and references to Appendices
LUCHEUX	1.10.18		36 Res. Pk. Section moved to LA FORIE FARM, 2 miles S. of LUCHEUX.	
do	2.10.18		Routine inspections of animals. Following animals were evacuated for sick	
do	3.10.18		during 3.10.18. From Division — 11, Mob. Vet. Sec. — 1.	
do	4.10.18			
do	5.10.18		36 Res. Pk. Section moved with Transport of Division to BOISLEUX-AU-MONT area. VICKARD V.S. XVII Corps at LOUVERAL.	
do	6.10.18		Divisional Headquarters moved to MOEUVRES (E.10.d. cent) 57 C. 36 Res. Pk. Section moved to D.10. a.9.b. (57C) XVII Corps V.E.S. at VAUX-VRAUCOURT.	
MOEUVRES	7.10.18		Visited Transport of Infantry B.N.s.	
do	8.10.18		1st Echelon Infantry Transport with V.O. V/e. A detachment of 36 M.V.S. Conducting 9/NEO. S.D. men left necessary driving supplies of equipment in great need. Charge of Capt. BURR R.V.C. attached to Headquarters. 73 Suffolks with draft St. Stephen took over 1st Echelon Infantry Transport. Location of detachment Mob. Vet. Section BOIS du NEUF.	
RUMILLY	9.10.18		Divisional Headquarters moved to MONT-SUR-L'OEVREL Achmumb Mob. Vet. Section moved S.W. of MERGNIES turning from to AWOINGT. During the evening 36 Mob. Pk. Section at GRAINCOURT, left owner to over to RUMILLY cab on morning of 10th.	
= Suburb of CAMBRAI	10.10.18		36 Res. Pk. Section at RUMILLY. Evacuation horses to XVII Corps V.E.S. at VAUX-VRAUCOURT, New Adv.V.S. Location opened V.E.S. opening. Vet. VI Corps V.E.S. near lair VELU. Lelz horse rear VI Corps V.E.S. would move	

Army Form C. 2118.

WAR DIARY
or
INTELLIGENCE SUMMARY.
(Erase heading not required.)

DADVS 4th DIVISION

Place	Date	Hour	Summary of Events and Information	Remarks and references to Appendices
Do	11.10.18		Return at MASNIERES on 12/10/18. Pilots Detachment 10th Vet. Section located at LA BABOTTE (B.4.a.2.0) (57 B). Ordered 36 Res. Vet. Section known coming to CAUROIR. Informed M.S. Vet. Section Francaise known to CAUROIR. Vet. evening. ADMS said that VES transferred at MARCOING on 17/10/18, asked that two TGs or all sick returnable evacuable then to MARCOING on 13/10/18, as known 36 Res. Vet. Section had a larger number of animals awaiting treatment than could be treated. Received 6 evacuable horses. VI Corps VES.	
Do	12.10.18.		Carg. morning of 12.10.18. Neilsa Detachment 10th M. Section located RIEUX, as it was rapidly moving forward following on 36 M.S. Vet. Section forward following as to AVESNES LEZ AUBERT. River Hyls. East to AVESNES LEZ AUBERT. 36 Res. Vet. Section at C4.6.5.8. (57 B.)	
Do	13.10.18			
AVESNES-LEZ-AUBERT	14.10.18		Inspected units.	
Do	15.10.18		Detached of 36 Mob. Vet. Section rejoined 36 Res. Vet. Section in rear Milij Meds Division by 4th Division.	

Army Form C. 2118.

WAR DIARY
or
INTELLIGENCE SUMMARY.
(Erase heading not required.)

D.A.D.V.S. 24th DIVISION

Place	Date	Hour	Summary of Events and Information	Remarks and references to Appendices
AVESNES-LEZ-AUBERT	6.10.18		24th Divisional Artillery at Cambrai. Hqrs he has been attached to 59th Division in Line Sectn. ADVS XVII Corps informed DVES hours move to CAMBRAI on arrival. DADVS cases arranged billets over the nit. occupied by 36 Mob. Vet Section.	
do	7.10.18		Reinsment to 36 Mob Vet Section known as 18th Mid Satellite	
do	18.10.18		Visited 19th Division Mob Vet Section at Cambrai. Divisional Headquarters moved to Cam. B Pat. Divisional Artillery moved to RIEUX.	
CAMBRAI	19.10.18		} Usual routine inspections.	
	20.10.18			
	21.10.18			
	22.10.18			
	23.10.18			
	24.10.18			
do	25.10.18		Seeing off Division had Division horses moved from Cambrai to Hqrs Lyphre Area. Detachment of 36 Mob. Vet Section attached to Capt J.R. Parker R.A.V.C. Reminder Charge of Capt. J.S. FAUBERT, 36 Mob Vet Section at	
STAUBERT	26.10.18		Divisional Headquarters at ST. AUBERT. Detachment 36 Mob Vet Section at HAUSSY.	

Army Form C. 2118.

WAR DIARY or INTELLIGENCE SUMMARY.

D.A.D.V.S. 94th DIVISION

(Erase heading not required.)

Place	Date	Hour	Summary of Events and Information	Remarks and references to Appendices
ST AUBERT	27.10.18 28.10.18 29.10.18 30.10.18 31.10.18		Veterinary Routine Inspection of animals. Having as the Principal Casualties during the week I.G. Gunshot Exhaustion 57 wounds. Debility 22 wounds I.S.R. wounds 4 Running Sores 1 Grooming sore 6, Rubbings 1 wounds. No new cases of mange. Numerous minor sore experience. Condition Numerous cases of mule stable lymph for one name. Chaff The chief cause. There was one condition. Equipping 2nd line Except special change by Clipping with manes. Horses Dry Sheared Coat work. Establishment Reduced by the Lieut. M. Nelson to Transit. Establishment that 2 are N.C.O.'s until late actions operation to 180 P. Until 2 are N.C.O.'s Equipment 16, out of these forming our respecs at follows. 2 stabler 1 Cook, 1 Storey Smith Equipment 1 cook leaving 9 for this service are 735 Ridr. 707 Veteri 1 army pt. 1 pt. box line 9. By arrange the Drivers 1 men 5 after 3 Post for transport. Establishment 1 Rec. 73 P. attached to 33 Mov. Battalion Foraging team. remains and on either. At present 3 Returning Evacuating Stations	

Army Form C. 2118.

WAR DIARY
or
INTELLIGENCE SUMMARY.

DADVS 9th DIVISION

(Erase heading not required.)

Place	Date	Hour	Summary of Events and Information	Remarks and references to Appendices
As located CAMBRAI.			b/Stabling lists DADVS 9th Division	

CONFIDENTIAL.

War Diary
of
D.A.D.V.S
24th DIVISION.

From 1-11-18.   To 30-11-18.

Vol. 39.

Army Form C. 2118.

WAR DIARY
or
INTELLIGENCE SUMMARY.

(Erase heading not required.)

D.A.D.V.S. 24th DIVISION

Place	Date	Hour	Summary of Events and Information	Remarks and references to Appendices
ST. AUBERT	1.11.18		Usual Routine.	
	2.11.18		Bde. Headquarters moved to BERMERAIN. 36 Mob. Veterinary Section to MAISON BLEUE on the VENDEGIES-SOLESMES road.	
do	3.11.18		Detachment of 36 Mob. Vet. Section attached to 75 L. of C. Infantry Transport located at LES FORRIERES (ST MARTIN) awaiting horse casualties. Infantry Transport detachment of 36 Mob. Vet. Sect. proceeded along SAULZOIR-VIKKERS POL road notifying horses.	
BERMERAIN	4.11.18		IVES traversed ST HILAIRE on 5th Cavd. Bde. Headquarters moved to SERMERIES. On reconnoitering SAULZOIR - VIKKERS POL road this Bde. found important detachment 36 Mob. Vet. Section had gone to SERMERIES. 36 Mob. Vet. Section located at MARECHES	
SERMERIES	5.11.18		Bde. Headquarters moved to WARGNIES, MARECHES, but also opened rest day Section moved to WARGNIES, St WAAST road. Detachment moved to GENIETTE to JENKAIN - ST WAAST road. WARGNIES - LE - PETIT.	
WARGNIES-LE-GRAND	6.11.18		Ran JENKAIN - LE PETIT. Visited Lt. Col. J. JENKAIN on the BAVAY road. In view of the casualties horses to be taken on/Studs persons relative or spare the Coffs of Horses/Studs persons relative or spare the Br "Q" as to the horse selection of Horse & Mules buffalo were instructed for casualties. V.D.S. instructed	

Army Form C. 2118.

WAR DIARY
or
INTELLIGENCE SUMMARY.
(Erase heading not required.)

DADVS. 24th DIVISION

Place	Date	Hour	Summary of Events and Information	Remarks and references to Appendices
WARGNIES-LE-GRAND	7.11.18		Detachment 36 Mob. Vet. Section moved to BAVAY. 36 Mob. Vet. Section moved to GENIETTE. by 36 Mob. Vet. Section for Watering. Number of animals evacuated from Division 63 V from other formations 50. 1st not Casualties in animals Diseases 67 Injuries/accidents 1st not P.C. Gunshot 115 (Killed 62 Enemy fire 50) Remaining 3 36 Mob. Vet. Section moved to ST WAAST-LA-VALLÉE	
do	8.11.18		36 Mob. Vet. Section moved to BAVAY. 36 Mob. Vet. Section Eastern outskirts. Office torn to enable army Vet. Services to function.	
do	9.11.18		BAVAY. a faction in Detachment 36 Mob. Vet. Section moved to the MONS road. LA BERLIERE. 17 V.E.S. too far away owing to Mob. Vet. Section left MAISON BLEUE - sufficient use not made of the Mob. Vet. Sections of Divisions in support. Present they would have been attached at slightly greater & rich back out but from forward Mob. Vet. Sections. 24th Division closure by 24th Division. Dvl. Veterinary moved to CHATEAU de RAMATZ. That part of BAVAY.	
BAVAY.	10.11.18		Dvl. Veterinary moved to V.E.S. near Station at BAVAY.	
do	11.11.18		36 Mob. Vet. Section moved to toning Attached reference 36 Mob. Vet. Section	

Army Form C. 2118.

WAR DIARY
or
INTELLIGENCE SUMMARY.
(Erase heading not required.)

DADVS 34th DIVISION

Place	Date	Hour	Summary of Events and Information	Remarks and references to Appendices
do.	12.11.18		Usual Routine. Wrote reminder for O/C 14th Fld.	
	13.11.18		Horse Show 18 from O/Ko. standing 31.	
	14.11.18		Admitted to VDAS Guard N° 45. (New 9. Evacuation 18 Remounts 2)	
	15.11.18		do. Division moved rest into DENAIN area — 1 Corps	
16.11.18			Other received Fd. Amb. Convalescent horse arrange for 36 hd. a.	
			First Army Supply Column also opening that month.	
			VH. Section horses also	
17.11.18			Inspected Remounts transfered from 61 st Division also 51 rd. to arrive	
			at CAUDRY. Division listed week to AUBERCHICOURT area. From	
			under VIII Corps.	
18.11.18			Post Headquarters moved to MASNY. 36 Rest Fd. Sebn. Coudre at LEWARDE.	
			talk Fld. Ambur.	
MASNY.	19.11.18		"	
	20.11.18		"	
	21.11.18		"	
	22.11.18		Usual Routine. Division Horse Show. 1 Copenener on 25th & 26th. 1st Final	
	23.11.18			
	24.11.18			
	25.11.18			
do.	26.11.18		All Arrangements made to SAMEON.	
SAMEON.	27.11.18		Usual Routine.	
	28.11.18			
	29.11.18			
	30.11.18			

W. Malone Major
DADVS 34th DIV.

CONFIDENTIAL.

War Diary

of

D.A.D.V.S.

24th Division.

From. 1-12-18.   To. 31-12-18.

Vol. 40.

Army Form C. 2118.

WAR DIARY
or
INTELLIGENCE SUMMARY
(Erase heading not required.)

D.A.D.V.S. 24th DIVISION.

Place	Date	Hour	Summary of Events and Information	Remarks and references to Appendices
SAMEON	1.12.18		Usual Routine.	
	2.12.18			
	3.12.18			
	4.12.18			
do	5.12.18		Inspected various H.T. selected as suitable for breeding purposes	
do	6.12.18		Lepuche mans belong to Brit. Artillery. H.T. selected for breeding R. Agnes	
do	7.12.18		Usual Routine. Section of horses for duty & sent to Capt J.H. Lewis Jones	
do	8.12.18		Sent Norman 11 Corps	
do	9.12.18		K Hersypoches. H.T. selected as suitable to breeding purposes	
do	10.12.18		Inspected horses Capt McKenna opinion operation	
do	11.12.18		Usual Routine.	
do	12.12.18		Col Haggard's horse to RONGY.	
RONGY	13.12.18		Usual Routine.	
do	14.12.18		Lepuche 203 Remount which arrived at RAISMES. Instructed V.O. to inoculate all aged animals on post induction from their own exchange	
do	15.12.18		Usual Routine.	
	16.12.18			
do	17.12.18		Attended 1st Corps Collection Committee on their inspection of mares likely to be suitable for breeding purposes	

Army Form C. 2118.

WAR DIARY
or
INTELLIGENCE SUMMARY
(Erase heading not required.)

DADVS 24th DIVISION

Place	Date	Hour	Summary of Events and Information	Remarks and references to Appendices
RONGY.	18.12.18		Divl. Headquarters moved to TOURNAI.	
TOURNAI	19.12.18		Usual Routine.	
	20.12.18			
	21.12.18			
	22.12.18			
	23.12.18		D.D.V.S. 1st Army visited No. 36 Mob. Vy. Section.	
	24.12.18			
do	25.12.18		Usual Routine.	
	26.12.18			
do	27.12.18		Instructions received from DVS. with reference to the classification	
	28.12.18		of animals for Demobilisation.	
	29.12.18			
do	30.12.18		Usual Routine.	
	31.12.18			

W.S. Hotchkiss Major
DADVS 24th Division

CONFIDENTIAL

WAR DIARY

of

D.A.D.V.S

24th DIVISION

FROM 1-1-19.   TO 31-1-19.

VOL 41.

D.A.D.V.S.
24th DIVISION.
No. Y1090
Date 14-3-19.

Army Form C. 2118

WAR DIARY
or
INTELLIGENCE SUMMARY
(Erase heading not required.)

D.A.D.V.S. 24th DIVISION

Instructions regarding War Diaries and Intelligence Summaries are contained in F.S. Regs., Part II. and the Staff Manual respectively. Title Pages will be prepared in manuscript.

Place	Date	Hour	Summary of Events and Information	Remarks and references to Appendices
TOURNAI.	1/1/19 2/1/19 3/1/19 4/1/19 5/1/19 6/1/19 7/1/19 8/1/19		Classification of war animals of Division by Board of Officers R.A.V.C. Belgian Truck Horses advised with all crossg feet & troth flaws & mange which occurs amongst civilian animals in Divl. area.	
	9/1/19 10/1/19 to 31/1/19		Inspected D/48 Bty R.F.A. on account of a outbreak of Sarcoptic mange. Classification of animals continued, also the kuling of all animals with mallein.	

[Signature]
D.A.D.V.S. 24th Division

CONFIDENTIAL

War Diary
of
D.A.D.V.S

24th Division

From 1-2-19.   To 28-2-19.

Vol. 42

D.A.D.V.S.
24th DIVISION.
No. Y.1090
Date 14-3-19.

Army Form C. 2118

WAR DIARY
or
INTELLIGENCE SUMMARY

D.A.D.V.S. 24th DIVISION

(Erase heading not required.)

Instructions regarding War Diaries and Intelligence Summaries are contained in F. S. Regs., Part II. and the Staff Manual respectively. Title Pages will be prepared in manuscript.

Place	Date	Hour	Summary of Events and Information	Remarks and references to Appendices
TOURNAI	1/2/19 to 19/2/19		Classification meeting Journals completed.	
	20/2/19		Orders issued as to the disposal of "C1" animals by sale to civilians by Public auction, arrangements made with local Auctioneer.	
	20/2/19 to 28/2/19		Election Journals for sales, supervision of sales.	

K. Ashra Maje
D.A.D.V.S. 24th Division